I0797783

"In this little but impactful book, Phil Ziegler continues his trail-blazing into a salient contemporary dogmatics of the apocalyptic gospel. He does so by daring to articulate an urgently needed but also carefully nuanced doctrine of the foe of God—the God whose end for the creation, breaking into the world in the event of Christ and its proclamation, is its redemption to righteousness, life, and peace. The deconstruction of the classical account of the devil as the fallen angel Lucifer for backing an implausible theodicy is alone worth the read. Even more impressive, however, is his better account of the evil one, known strictly as the adversary of Christ in the very process of its defeat in principle, if not yet fully in power."

—PAUL R. HINLICKY, *Distinguished Professor and Research Fellow, Christ Seminary of the Institute of Lutheran Theology*

"Although the subject of the devil is widely neglected in modern theology, our culture continues to adopt the concept of the demonic in the face of grotesque manifestations of evil. Philip Ziegler's perceptive study offers a constructive though chastened theological account of such language. As a vital 'ontological metaphor,' discourse about the diabolic cannot be avoided, he argues, if we are to sustain an adequate account of redemption, sin, and evil. This is likely to prove the most important work on the subject in a long time."

—DAVID FERGUSSON, *Regius Professor of Divinity, University of Cambridge*

"This is a brilliant book. Coming from the Reformed tradition, which has often been hesitant to discuss the devil, Phil Ziegler relocates the theology of the devil in the second article instead of the first: the devil is Christ's adversary rather than a creature gone wrong. This recalibration evidently fits the biblical witness better than the traditional approach did. Ziegler retrieves the language of cosmic battle in the synoptic gospels, shedding fresh light on Jesus Christ as the Way, Truth, and Life along the way. The readable, often humorous, style matches the content: while ultimate evil is very serious, Christ's victory puts it in perspective. This book is a fine example of the creative power of systematic theological thinking. It is a must-read for all who are interested in the power of evil—and Christ's victory over it."

—ARNOLD HUIJGEN, *Professor of Dogmatics, Protestant Theological University, Utrecht, The Netherlands*

"Baptismal vows frequently include the renunciation of the devil, but Christian reflection on that figure often begins and ends there. In these pages Philip Ziegler discloses the necessity of taking the devil seriously in any account of salvation. His proposal is as well-informed by the Gospels and the theological tradition as it is urgently needed. *God's Adversary and Ours* is a major contribution."

—BEVERLY ROBERTS GAVENTA, *Helen H. P. Manson Professor of New Testament Literature and Exegesis Emerita, Princeton Theological Seminary*

"This book is at once daring and necessary. It confronts an aspect of the Scriptural witness that has been suppressed within large parts of the tradition, and the Reformed tradition in particular: the presence and activity of the devil. In doing so it invites a profound rethinking of the traditional Christian landscape and our place within it. Critiquing the domestication of the devil under the auspices of the doctrine of providence, Ziegler calls us from a cool, third person stance towards evil to a first person resistance of the devil in the prayerful working out of our salvation. This call entails, moreover, a radical recasting of the role of doctrine more broadly."

—SUSANNAH TICCIATI, *Professor of Christian Doctrine, King's College London*

"Christian thinking about the devil can range from the wacky to the waved-by. Is there any purpose or promise in writing a responsible diabology? Emphatically, yes, says Philip Ziegler! Clarity about the nature of the good news demands it. The gospel proclaims that Jesus is the way, the life, and the truth, but a powerful adversary opposes Jesus and his mission with temptation, oppression, and falsehood. Central to the good news of God's redemption is Jesus's struggle with and final defeat of God's adversary and ours, the devil. With wit, wisdom, and winsomeness, Ziegler has given us a book on the devil destined to become a classic."

—DOUGLAS HARINK, *Professor Emeritus of Theology, The King's University*

PHILIP G. ZIEGLER

GOD'S ADVERSARY AND OURS

A Brief Theology of the Devil

BAYLOR UNIVERSITY PRESS

Cover and book design by Elyxandra Encarnación
Cover image: Rembrandt van Rijn, A sketch of the devil (Satan) tempting Jesus Christ following his forty days of fasting in the wilderness, 1640–1642. Wikimedia Commons, public domain.

The Library of Congress has cataloged this book under ISBN 978-1-4813-2413-7.

Library of Congress Control Number: 2025939702

Helena, for aye

CONTENTS

PREFACE AND ACKNOWLEDGMENTS

This little book has its origins in the Annie Kinkead Warfield Lectures delivered at Princeton Theological Seminary in March 2024. It was a great privilege to be invited to take up the lectureship. I am grateful to Bruce McCormack who in his role then as Hodge Professor of Theology made the nomination, and to the seminary's faculty as a whole for its willingness in turn to support it. It was a privilege to engage with the students and faculty of the seminary during the week I was resident in their community to deliver them. I remain indebted to Dr. Kaitlyn Dugan, Director of the Center for Barth Studies, together with all the other Seminary staff who saw to the preparations and all the various practical arrangements the lectures involved with such professionalism, care, and consideration.

I was delighted to discover that other "Aberdeen Divines" have previously delivered Warfield Lectures: first J. K. S. Reid (1959–60) and latterly also James B. Torrance (2000–2001). The Divinity department of the University of Aberdeen has to this day many good and fruitful connections with Princeton Theological Seminary: some of our faculty and students are alums; many of us count seminary faculty as close professional colleagues and co-conspirators in our fields. For myself, the year I spent as a postdoctoral fellow at Princeton University largely holed up in the special collections of the Seminary's wondrous library studying Paul L. Lehmann's archived papers and thinking about the nature of Christian theology and ethics was a rich and formative time for which I remain ever grateful.

I hope that publication of these Warfield Lectures may make a real if modest contribution toward enhancing our contemporary theological conversation about the promises and claims of the Christian gospel and its manifold entailments. I further hope that this volume might, by both its content and its form, also serve to "advance some doctrine or doctrines of the Reformed System of Doctrine" and thereby honor the specific ends to which the Annie Kinkead Warfield lectureship is committed.

The origins of this study reach back many years into conversations arising from the exploration of the significance of developments in Pauline exegesis—specifically those sometimes referred to as "the apocalyptic Paul"—for Christian doctrine. I am grateful to my biblical and theological colleagues in the ad hoc "Explorations in Theology and Apocalyptic" group for their fellowship and conversation along the way. A special thanks to the Aberdeen Divinity postgraduate students who diligently participated in what we came to call "Satan's Own Seminar" in 2023–24 for their willingness to read and to think together about this unusual theme, and for their very valuable feedback and contributions which helped to shape the lectures themselves. Several colleagues—Paul Nimmo, Beverly Gaventa, Susannah Ticciati, Paul Hinlicky, Kaitlyn Dugan, Declan Kelly—also generously took the time to read and comment upon the original manuscripts of the lectures, and I am very grateful to them for all their insightful criticisms, questions, and suggestions. It goes without saying that whatever continues to disappoint them and other readers here is entirely down to me.

I am much obliged to Dr. David Nelson of Baylor University Press, together with all his editorial team, for all their encouragement and efforts in bringing this volume into print.

1
SATAN—
A MOTIVATIONAL TALK

> Rarely is anything said in our day about the demonic.[1]
>
> Søren Kierkegaard

"A CALVINIST AND A JESUIT WALK INTO A BAR . . .": POSITIONING THE PROBLEM

A story to begin.[2]

Ostrog, Poland, 1627. A Calvinist noblewoman is beset by the devil, perhaps even possessed. The local Calvinists, we are told, "did not have the courage to attempt to cure her" and so brought her to the rector of the local Jesuit seminary. The rector initially rebuffed them, insisting that they should "send for [their] own ministers and schismatic priests and see what power they have over the devil." The Calvinists baulked, admitting "that their ministers did not possess the power to cast out demons." Relenting, the rector visited the woman and discerned she was indeed possessed. Then, it is reported:

1 Søren Kierkegaard, *The Concept of Anxiety*, ed. and trans. Reidar Thomte (Princeton University Press, 1980), 118.

2 The following is taken from Antonio Francesco Mariani, *The Life of St. Ignatius Loyola, Founder of the Jesuits*, 2 vols. (Thomas Richardson and Son, 1849), 2:356–60; reproduced in Paul Thigpen, *Saints Who Battled Satan* (TAN Books, 2015), 116–19.

> As the rector was even more eager to heal the souls of the Calvinists than the body of the woman, he instructed them to bring a book of Calvin's *Institutes*, or some other book containing their own dogmas and give it to the woman. This was accordingly done, and the Devil began to kiss and caress it with great marks of joy. The rector then took it and hid a picture of St. Ignatius between the pages; then he presented it to her again. The demon drew back, screaming with anger and would not even touch it.

At this "the Calvinists were greatly confounded." Eventually, the rector exorcises the noblewoman by invoking the power of "Mary and Ignatius" and, in the end, we read that she "solemnly renounced her errors and professed the Catholic faith." Tidy.

This curious little tale intimates that our Reformed forebears were largely at a loss as regards the devil and his works. The original storyteller rather uncharitably chalks this up to moral cowardice, spiritual weakness, liturgical incompetence, and heretical doctrine. Yet, even reading past the (almost playful) polemics, the suggestion remains: even if the devil is rather fond of Calvin's *Institutes*, Calvinists themselves just do not do the devil, really.

We might readily imagine why. Think first of the range of historic Reformed doctrinal distinctives which conspire against giving much scope to the idea of the devil: unimpeded divine sovereignty, exhaustive providence, rigorously forensic accounts of salvation within a strong bilateral covenant, the embrace of believers' spiritual struggles within the firm assurance of preservation of the elected saints, not to mention a deep Protestant wariness of superstition. To this we might add the strong sense of human responsibility and demystifying impulse that marks much modern Reformed theology and ethics: deeply worried about exculpatory appeals to the devil as a cause of human sin, Reformed faith and life has resolutely resisted invocation of the *diabolus ex machina*, we might say.

Furthermore, as regards the nature of the "evil" we actually confront in the life of faith, many of us will readily agree with the view recently expressed by theologian Jacqueline daCosta when she writes:

> How then to define evil in the twenty-first century? I reject the fiction of a metaphysical entity and hold responsible an historic accumulation of human errors; belief systems that created a god in their own image; scientists who seek short-term solutions that result in

> long-term disasters, or do not question how their research will be used; politicians that force ideologies on us that suit only a fraction of the population at the expense of the majority; a majority that would rather play with their toys than question where technology is leading them. It is the systemic failure of civilization that is the root of today's evils.[3]

How could talk of the devil ever find a place alongside such critical analysis of human malfeasance and its systemic accretion over time? As Jürgen Moltmann observes, "the 'devil' is a mythical figure used to pin down fear in the face of the monstrous. . . . It has no explanatory significance in the modern, scientific-technological civilization."[4] But just because this is so does not mean folks won't try it on, of course. As Miguel De La Torre and Albert Hernández argue in *The Quest for the Historical Satan*, invocation of the devil today plays to our desire to oversimplify the enormous complexities involved in the workings of unjust structures and systems. They write, "the illusion of Satan as the father of all evil not only excuses and absolves God of any responsibility for evil but also excuses and absolves those with power and privilege who benefit from the status quo that causes suffering for many who reside on the margins of society."[5] It seems the devil is and remains the enemy of moral seriousness.

For reasons then both orthodox and modern, metaphysical and moral, our Reformed theology generally has and continues to be encouraged to *bypass* the devil. Already in the early nineteenth century Friedrich Schleiermacher gave voice to the view that Reformed theology is properly "as little concerned to dispute the concept of the devil as to establish it."[6] It is totally unsurprising, then, that in a recent ecumenical symposium about the topic, Cynthia Rigby honestly admits that one simply does not hear much if any talk about the demonic, the devil, and the powers and principalities in Presbyterian

[3] Jacqueline daCosta, "Evil in the Twenty-First Century," *Feminist Theology* 30, no. 2 (2022): 177.

[4] Jürgen Moltmann, "Zwölf Bemerkungen zur Symbolik des Bösen," *Evangelische Theologie* 52, no. 1 (1992): 2 (translation mine).

[5] Miguel A. De La Torre and Albert Hernández, *The Quest for the Historical Satan* (Fortress, 2011), 198.

[6] F. D. E. Schleiermacher, *The Christian Faith*, trans. H. R. Mackintosh (T&T Clark, 1928), section 1, §45.

churches today.[7] That reticence, as we have seen, may be for very good reasons indeed.

The devil, then, might seem a deeply unpromising theme, especially for an author looking to advance "some doctrine or doctrines of the Reformed System of Doctrine" as Warfield lecturers are obliged to attempt.[8] But allow me to try to convince you otherwise.

SOME POSSIBLE MOTIVATIONS FOR REVISITING THE DEVIL

Reflect for a moment about some things that might motivate one, if not warmly to embrace "the devil and all his works," then at least to be open to revisiting the theme as a topic in contemporary Reformed theology.

Cultural Motivations

We might begin by reflecting on the presence of the devil in considered cultural discourse about evil in the twentieth century and beyond. As Canadian novelist David Adams Richards writes, an honest gaze upon our recent history—on scales both large and small—should convince us that "We know we have existed in a world where evil sparkles."[9] The scale, depth, and seeming incompressibility of evil and of human suffering manifest in modernity—for which the transatlantic slave trade, the unprecedented experiences of total warfare of the First and Second World Wars, the Holocaust of European Jewry, and the atomic annihilation of the cities of Hiroshima and Nagasaki, are often powerful symbolic shorthands and synecdoches—has led some of our

7 Cynthia L. Rigby, "Evil and the Principalities: Disarming the Demonic," in *Life amid the Principalities: Identifying, Understanding, and Engaging Created, Fallen, and Disarmed Powers Today*, ed. Michael Root and James J. Buckley, Pro Ecclesia 6 (Wipf and Stock, 2016), 51 (51–67).

8 From the correspondence of the seminary's "Administrative Committee," 1957, concerning the stipulated terms of the endowment from the Warfield estate: "(c) That the subject of the lectures shall in all cases be some doctrine or doctrines of the Reformed System of Doctrine, and shall deal either with the Biblical Basis, or the Historical Development, or the Systematic formulation of the Exposition or Defense of said doctrine or doctrines."

9 David Adams Richards, "I Will Show You Fear in a Handful of Dust," *Vision: A Journal for Church and Theology* 20, no. 1 (2019): 30.

best intellects to near despair.[10] Ours is a world in which barbarity keeps ready company with civility, sadism and technological acuity happily clasp hands, and nihilistic stupidity repeatedly masquerades as wisdom. These experiences conspire to deflate progressive hopes and to corrode confidence in the deliverances of our late modern civilizations. The experience of evil in our age has given birth to "modern Manichaeans," thinkers who find it easy to imagine that our world has been abandoned by God, but impossible to think it abandoned by Satan.[11] These thinkers discern our world to be a bedeviled world deserted by divine goodness, a world whose "whole entire being—flesh, blood, sensibility, intelligence, love" appears to have been handed over "to the pitiless necessity of matter and the cruelty of the devil," as Simone Weil once wrote.[12]

More narrowly, we might consider how honest confrontation of the evils of our age drives people to reach for the language of the demonic in their attempts to do justice to the reality of the world they face. Speaking in 2015, Michiko Kodama, a *Hibakusha*—i.e., a survivor of the 1945 atomic bombings—spoke plainly of nuclear weapons as "weapons of the devil which cannot coexist with humans."[13] Her sentiment was eerily anticipated by the scientists who nicknamed the third experimental fissile plutonium core engineered for the Manhattan Project "The Demon Core"—a compressed, annihilating power that silently poisoned all those who circled around in its demanding service. Or consider the Jewish philosopher Emil Fackenheim, who, looking long into the abyss of the *Shoah*, discerned there a transcendent, unsurpassable, and absolute evil, an "eruption of demonism into history."[14]

[10] As Susan Neiman remarks, if the Lisbon earthquake "marked the moment of recognition that traditional theodicy was hopeless, Auschwitz signalled the recognition that every replacement fared no better." Susan Neiman, *Evil in Modern Thought* (Princeton University Press, 2002), 281.

[11] Zygmunt Bauman and Leonidas Donskis, *Liquid Evil* (Polity, 2016), 2.

[12] Simone Weil, *First and Last Notebooks*, trans. Richard Reese (Oxford University Press, 1970), 103.

[13] "Weapons of the Devil: Hibakusha's Call for a World Without Nuclear Weapons," *American Friends Service Committee*, August 5, 2015, https://afsc.org/news/weapons-devil-hibakushas-call-world-without-nuclear-weapons.

[14] For discussion see Laurie McRobert, "Emil L. Fackenheim and Radical Evil: Transcendent, Unsurpassable, Absolute," *Journal of the American Academy of Religion* 58, no. 2 (1989): 325–40.

Again the devil appears in such speech as a "necessary metaphor" to represent "realities, i.e., magnitudes of evil in history, which cannot be expressed any other way"; indeed, as Kenneth Green's recent study of Fackenheim's thinking concludes, for him the Holocaust finally proved to be nothing less than a "diabolical revelation," something pressing far beyond the mere "eclipse of God."[15]

So, too, do Jean-Luc Marion's riveting phenomenological reflections on the violent, vengeful, and evasive logic of evil climax, perhaps surprisingly, in direct contemplation of the figure of Satan, his uncanny being and his self-obscuring action. For Marion the figure of the devil proves crucial to grasping the true nature of the destructive reality of evil precisely because it manifests "its intention and its essence."[16] A similar philosophical approach leads Philippe Nemo's profound study of Job's suffering to an account of evil that sees it marked by both transcendent excess and intention.[17] Such sentiments are echoed in Adam Kotsko's judgment that our disastrous contemporary order "is surely demonic, endlessly flapping its wings to keep itself irrevocably stuck in the place, interminably consuming its victims without ever being satisfied."[18] The recurrent rediscovery in America of William Stringfellow's arresting "political demonology" and its continuing pertinence reflects a discerning sense of the relevance, even necessity, of recourse to such theological concepts in order to do justice to what is "really going on" around us.[19]

The intuition at work in all these cases is that something important is gained by such invocations of the devil, that we win some new and crucial purchase on our reality through such redescriptions which otherwise cannot be had. Talk of the devil here affords traction on a

[15] Kenneth Hart Green, *The Philosophy of Emil Fackenheim: From Revelation to the Holocaust* (Cambridge University Press, 2020), 277, 271, and ch. 8, "Diabolical Revelation and the Holocaust," 269–317. The phrase "eclipse of God" here comes from Martin Buber, *The Eclipse of God: Studies in the Relation of Religion and Philosophy* (Harper & Row, 1952).

[16] Jean-Luc Marion, "Evil in Person," in *Prolegomena to Charity*, trans. Stephen E. Lewis (Fordham University Press, 2002), 23.

[17] Philippe Nemo, *Job and the Excess of Evil* (Duquesne University Press, 1998) and discussion in Emmanuel Levinas, "Transcendence and Evil," in *Of God Who Comes to Mind*, trans. Bettina Bergo (Stanford University Press, 1998), 122–34.

[18] Adam Kotsko, *The Prince of this World* (Stanford University Press, 2017), 206.

[19] Most recently see Matt Loftin, "Political Demons," *Christian Century* 142, no. 2 (2025).

feature of our reality which would otherwise elude us, forms of evil at once banal *and* unfathomable, highly rationalized *and* absurd, excessive *and* effective. It calls out the absurdity, inexplicability, scope and depth and power and nullity of evil, its outworking as the seemingly overwhelming contradiction of life, of meaning, of truth. It is essential that we must grasp how recourse to such "demonic poetics"[20]—i.e., to "ontological metaphors" for evil, as Beverly Gaventa has called them—seeks not to remystify but actually to *demystify* the world, i.e., to help us catch sight of something real about our situation, something which would otherwise always remain just out of view, just beyond the edges of the frame.[21]

Ecumenical Motivations

While it may seem odd to say, interest in the devil might well also be one of the things Reformed faith and theology can receive from other Christian traditions in what my teacher Margaret O'Gara characterized as our ongoing "ecumenical gift exchange."[22] Perhaps even in our current "ecumenical winter" our sisters and brothers in the faith will be glad to share something of the devil with their Reformed cousins.

Lutheranism certainly presents its Protestant neighbor with a heightened interest in the devil, beginning of course with Luther's own intense fascination with the fiend.[23] Gustav Wingren's charge

[20] "Demonic poetics" is a phrase taken from Edward Simon, *Pandemonium: A Visual History of the Devil* (Abrams/Cernunnos, 2022).

[21] Beverly Gaventa, "The Rhetoric of Violence and the God of Peace in Paul's Letter to the Romans," in *Paul, John and Apocalyptic Eschatology*, ed. Jan Krans et al. (Brill, 2013), 73. She is adapting an idiom from Jeffrey Burton Russell, *A History of Heaven: The Singing Silence* (Princeton University Press, 1997), 8: "Metaphorical ontology is the use of figures of speech to go beyond science, history, and poetry . . . more than illustrative figures of speech or vivid personifications [ontological metaphors] are attempts to grasp in language a reality that is beyond language . . ."

[22] Margaret O'Gara, *The Ecumenical Gift Exchange* (Liturgical, 1998).

[23] See comprehensively Harmannus Obendiek, *Der Teufel bei Martin Luther* (Furche Verlag, 1931) and most recently Daniel Mühlethaler, *Der Teufel wider den trinitarischen Gott in der Theologie Martin Luthers* (Evangelische Verlangsanstalt, 2024). In a more biographical mode is the famous study of Heiko Oberman, *Luther: Man Between God and the Devil*, trans. Eileen Walliser-Schwarzbart (Yale University Press, 1989). Concisely see Hans-Martin Barth, *Der Teufel und Jesus Christus in der Theologie Martin Luthers* (Vandenhoeck & Ruprecht, 1967), and still more concisely "Zur inneren Entwicklung von Luthers Teufelglauben," *Kerygma und Dogma* 13 (1967): 201–11.

against Karl Barth's theology—namely, that it had no scope of the devil—reflects a distinctive Lutheran concern for the lively, existential struggle with sin supported by diabology.[24] The afflictions of *tentatio* or *Anfechtung*—that agonizing inner struggle against doubt and despair before God which Luther suggested as one of the keys to the making of a theologian—were assigned unambiguously to the work of the devil by the reformer. There is, he suggested, no real faith or serious theological understanding which is not won through relentless struggle against the harrying of the devil.[25] This sensibility is also echoed in the work of modern Lutheran theologians like Gustaf Aulén, who argues in his famous work, *Christus Victor*, that the victorious defeat of the devil by Christ should be acknowledged and honored as the truly "classic" account of salvation; so, too, in the writings of Helmut Thielicke, whose preaching and theology both make much of the devil as a crucial theme precisely for *modern* faith. Writing in 1943, Thielicke remarked matter-of-factly that "*Anybody who would understand history must in be possession of the category of the demonic.*"[26]

To this we might also add impulses from Roman Catholicism. While a contested subject in modern Roman Catholic theology to be sure, formal teaching since Vatican II has reaffirmed the traditional teaching on demonology.[27] Renewal in 1999 of the major rite of exorcism—*De exorcismis et supplicationibus quibusdam* ("On Exorcisms and Other Supplications")—and the related reassertion of the role and training of diocesan exorcists suggests that liturgical and

[24] Gustav Wingren, *Theology in Conflict: Nygren, Barth, Bultmann*, trans. E. H. Wahlstrom (Muhlenberg Press, 1958), 25.

[25] On the threefold formative experience of *oratio, meditatio, tentatio* see Martin Luther, *The Career of the Reformer IV*, vol. 34 of *Luther's Works*, ed. and trans. Lewis W. Spitz (Muhlenberg Press, 1960), 285.

[26] Helmut Thielicke, "The Reality of the Demonic," in *Man in God's World: The Faith and Courage to Live—or Die*, trans. J. W. Doberstein (James Clarke, 1967), 166 (163–98); original German, "Über die Wircklichkeit des Dämonischen. Das Geheimnis der Überpersönlichen Mächte," in *Fragen des Christentums an die Moderne Welt* (Mohr, 1947), 170–217. See also Gustaf Aulén, *Christus Victor: An Historical Study of the Three Main Types of the Idea of the Atonement*, trans. A. G. Herbert (SPCK, 1931).

[27] Most directly the Vatican document "Christian Faith and Demonology," *L'Osservatore Romano*, English ed., July 10, 1975, 6–10, as well as *The Catechism of the Catholic Church*, 2nd ed. (United States Council of Catholic Bishops, 2019), §§391–95, pp. 98–99, on "The Fall of the Angels," which rehearses the received view concisely.

pastoral attention to the devil and all his works remains a notable feature of contemporary Roman Catholic faith and life worldwide.[28] The readiness of Pope Francis to speak plainly and frequently of the devil has been newsworthy. In his formal teaching on the subject, Pope Francis explicitly stressed that "we should not think of the devil as a myth, a representation, a symbol, a figure of speech or an idea" but "as a personal being who assails us."[29]

Eastern Orthodox soteriology has always emphasized Christ's work of redemption from the condition of the fall and the captivity to death which besets it. Such emphasis upon sin as a condition of ontic corruption—i.e., of creaturely life depleted by death—makes the trope of the defeat of death as an inimical power central to the idea of salvation; so, too, then liberation from corruption and the renewal of creaturely being in the image of God. As John of Damascus summarized classically, Christ saves by "communication of life" which "delivers us from corruption" so that God "might redeem us from the tyranny of the devil, and might strengthen and teach us how to overthrow the tyrant through patience and humility."[30] Interestingly, the devil explicitly plays an outsized role in some of the most formative sources of this tradition—e.g., in the Cappadocians and John Chrysostom—something recent scholarship by Gabrielle Thomas and others is helping us to appreciate anew.[31]

[28] See Fintan Lyons, OSB, *The Persistence of Evil: A Cultural, Literary and Theological Analysis* (T&T Clark, 2023), 247–305. For an insightful journalistic account of contemporary interest in exorcism and related practices see John Thavis, *The Vatican Prophecies: Investigating Supernatural Signs, Apparitions, and Miracles in the Modern Age* (Viking, 2015), esp. ch. 4, "Full of the Devil." For theological reflection on an (in)famous instance of Catholic exorcism in Germany in the 1970s see Manfred Adler et al., *Tod und Teufel in Klingenberg: Eine Dokumentation* (Paul Pattloch Verlag, 1977).

[29] Pope Francis, *Gaudete et Exsultate* (March 19, 2018), esp. §§160–61, https://www.vatican.va/content/francesco/en/apost_exhortations/documents/papa-francesco_esortazione-ap_20180319_gaudete-et-exsultate.html.

[30] John of Damascus, *On the Orthodox Faith*, vol. 3 of *The Fount of Knowledge*, trans. Norman Russell (St. Vladimir's Seminary Press, 2022), 4.20.

[31] Gabrielle Thomas, *The Image of God in the Theology of Gregory of Nazianzus* (Cambridge University Press, 2019), esp. ch. 4, "The *imago dei* and the Devil," 87–117, as well her recent essay "Basil of Caesarea and Gregory of Nazianzus on the Role of the Devil in Problems of Evil and Suffering," *International Journal of Systematic Theology* 26, no. 4 (2024): 351–66. See also Samantha L. Miller, *Chrysostom's Devil: Demons, The Will, and Virtue in Patristic Soteriology* (IVP Academic, 2020).

Meanwhile in Britain, one finds that both the Church of England and Methodists have well-established and formalized "deliverance ministry" networks for which they supply official theological and liturgical resources.[32] Perhaps this ought not to be surprising. After all, it was John Wesley who is said to have formulated the bold evangelical axiom: "No devil, no God."[33] Certainly no library of demonology will want to be without a copy of that most winsomely English of exorcism manuals entitled *Those Tiresome Intruders* penned by the retired bishop of Carlisle.[34]

Last—but not least to be sure—surging global Pentecostalism today raises the question of the devil in relation to its widespread practices of deliverance. As Esther Acolatse—a self-described "Reformed Presbycostal"—argues, a frank reckoning with these matters is essential to any open theological encounter between global south and global north in our time.[35] The prominence of the devil in Pentecostalism has, in fact, greatly expanded over the decades: its earlier significance as a discrete obstacle to charismatic healing has now been overtaken by the devil's central place in the widespread discourse and practice of "spiritual warfare."[36] The expansive impact of the latter in shaping the life and ministry of the most rapidly expanding charismatic Christian communities around the globe is a phenomenon not to be ignored, even—and perhaps especially—if one is uncertain quite how best to understand and appreciate it.[37]

[32] See https://www.churchofengland.org/safeguarding/safeguarding-e-manual/safeguarding-children-young-people-and-vulnerable-adults/section-41-deliverance-ministry and https://www.methodist.org.uk/for-churches/governance/faith-and-order/guidelines-for-deliverance-ministry/.

[33] Cited in Neil Forsyth, *The Old Enemy: Satan & the Combat Myth* (Princeton University Press, 1987), 7–8.

[34] Graham Dow, *Those Tiresome Intruders: Sharing Experience in the Ministry of Deliverance* (Grove Books, 1991); repr. as *Explaining Deliverance* (Sovereign World, 2003).

[35] Esther E. Acolatse, *Powers, Principalities and the Spirit: Biblical Realism in Africa and the West* (Eerdmans, 2018).

[36] Opoku Onyinah, "Spiritual Warfare: The Cosmic Conflict Between Good and Evil," in *The Routledge Handbook of Pentecostal Theology*, ed. Wolfgang Vondley (Routledge, 2020), 321–31.

[37] For example, David L. Bradnick, *Evil, Spirits, and Possession: An Emergentist Theology of the Demonic*, Global Pentecostal and Charismatic Studies 25 (Brill, 2017).

Taken together, one might receive these provocative "gifts" offered from every ecumenical quarter as a collective invitation to think again about the devil as an element of Reformed faith and doctrine.

Biblical Motivations

But what of biblical motivations? Whatever else Reformed theology may be it is certainly a manner of theology insistent upon being exposed to fresh hearings and better readings of the biblical witness to the gospel of Jesus Christ. Now, none of the Gospels, or the Acts of the Apostles, or any of Paul's or other epistles collected in the New Testament, not even the book of Revelation, is properly *about* the devil, i.e., none of these texts have the devil as their chief and proper subject matter. Yet, the gospel of Jesus Christ which—in all its various attestations—*is* their true concern cannot, it seems, be told, reported, recorded, expressed, explained, exposited, and attested without talk of the devil.[38] When we hear the gospel as news in the mouths of the New Testament witnesses, we hear together with it reports of the devil and his works.[39] As you might imagine, industrious biblical scholars have not left this matter untreated. I shall be interacting with and drawing upon a good body of this exegetical scholarship over the course of subsequent chapters of this book. But for now, let me just make two motivating observations.

The first is that, as Thomas Farrar and Guy Williams have shown in a series of recent studies and "inventories," there is a surfeit of "diabolical data" distributed across the strata and breadth of the earliest Christian literature.[40] The devil is consistently present

[38] For summary discussion see representatively Jeffrey Burton Russell, *The Devil: Perceptions of Evil from Antiquity to Primitive Christianity* (Cornell University Press, 1977), 221–49, and *Evil and the Devil*, ed. Ida Fröhlich and Erkki Koskenniemi (T&T Clark, 2013).

[39] See Christopher Morse, *The Difference Heaven Makes: Rehearing the Gospel as News* (T&T Clark, 2010).

[40] Thomas J. Farrar and Guy J. Williams, "Diabolical Data: A Critical Inventory of New Testament Satanology," *Journal for the Study of the New Testament* 39, no. 1 (2016): 40–71; Thomas J. Farrar and Guy J. Williams, "Talk of the Devil: Unpacking the Language of New Testament Satanology," *Journal for the Study of the New Testament* 39, no. 1 (2016): 72–96; Thomas J. Farrar, "The Intimate and Ultimate Adversary: Satanology in Early Second-Century Christian Literature," *Journal of Early Christian Studies* 26, no. 4 (2018): 517–46; Thomas J. Farrar, "New Testament Satanology and Leading Superhuman Opponents in Second Temple Jewish Literature: A Religio-

and regularly "topical"—i.e., more than merely incidental—in New Testament texts. Compared to the striking paucity of reference in the Old Testament, this early Christian discourse about the devil is rich and expansive. When compared with the exuberant variety of wider Second Temple literature it also stands out as reasonably consolidated and quite coherent. The New Testament texts, as Loren Stuckenbruck observes, show "remarkable unanimity in attributing manifestations of evil to a single figure" under the interchangeable designators "Satan," "the devil," and "the evil one."[41] All this suggests that "something is up" in these texts, something which invites further investigation and explanation in both historical and theological registers, something which may not actually be reflected in our doctrine as it should.

Second, beyond the impression made by the scale and distribution of the data are the striking *programmatic formulations* which summarize the gospel of salvation in ways which explicitly involve talk of the devil. For example, writing in Acts, Luke compresses the gospel into the report that "[Jesus] went about doing good and healing all who were oppressed by the devil" (Acts 10:38). Paul summarizes his own ministry in similar terms in Acts 26:18. Readers of Hebrews are instructed that since we are creatures of flesh and blood, Christ "likewise shared the same things, so that through death he might destroy the one who has the power of death, that is, the devil, and free those who all their lives were held in slavery by the fear of death" (Heb 2:14–15). And 1 John sums up the entire gospel message in these few words: "The Son of God was revealed for this purpose: to destroy the works of the devil" (1 John 3:8). It seems that the gospel of salvation is liable to repeated and dense restatement in explicitly diabolical terms.

Historical Analysis," *Journal of Theological Studies* NS 70, no. 1 (2019): 21–68. Cf. Tom de Bruin, "In Defence of New Testament Satanologies: A Response to Farrar and Williams," *Journal for the Study of the New Testament* 44, no. 3 (2022): 435–51.

[41] Loren T. Stuckenbruck, "Satan and Demons," in *Jesus Among Friends and Enemies: A Historical and Literary Introduction to Jesus in the Gospels*, ed. Chris Keith and Larry W. Hurtado (Baker Academic, 2011), 181, which also gives full lists of NT citations for all three "names." See also Derek R. Brown, "The Devil in the Details: A Survey of Research on Satan on Biblical Studies," *Currents in Biblical Research* 9, no. 2 (2011): 200–227.

Not only is the central object of Christian *faith* expressed in this way, but the substance of Christian *hope* is also regularly expressed with reference to the devil as, for example, in 1 Corinthians 15, Revelation 20, and jarringly in Romans 16 when Paul promises his readers that "the God of peace will shortly crush Satan under your feet."[42] Furthermore, the apostolic witnesses also regularly characterize the Christian *life* in agonistic terms as a confrontation with the devil: "Discipline yourselves; keep alert" comes the counsel, for "Like a roaring lion your adversary the devil prowls around, looking for someone to devour. *Resist him* . . ." (1 Pet 5:8–9). Famously, the whole armory of faith, righteousness, truth, peace, Word, and Spirit is required if one is "to stand against the wiles of the devil, for our struggle is not against blood and flesh but against the rulers, against the authorities, against the cosmic powers of this present darkness, against the spiritual forces of evil in the heavenly places" (Eph 6:11–12). That the devil is firmly ingredient in such striking expressions of primitive Christian faith, Christian hope, and Christian life stands as a further provocation to readers and preachers of these texts and to the theologians whose critical reflection aims to serve them.

Motivations from the Apocalyptic Paul

I myself have another particular biblical motivation for this venture to take up the devil as a theme in Christian dogmatics. For many years now I have been an avid if amateur student of contemporary debates in Pauline studies, cultivating a particular interest in the so-called "apocalyptic Paul."[43] A line of interpretation pioneered by Ernst Käsemann, J. Louis Martyn, J. Christiaan Beker and advanced today in the work of Beverly Gaventa, Susan Eastman, Alexandra Brown, Martinus de Boer, and others, this reading of Paul takes particular note of the cosmic framing of his gospel, its construal of Jesus Christ as the upending advent of God's saving power, and of Christ's death and resurrection as the effective "turning of the ages," i.e., the passing away of the old and the inauguration of the new creation. Fundamentally, this approach looks to identify and honor the central concern of Paul's gospel: namely, in the words of Donald MacKinnon, the power and urgency of "God's own protest

[42] 1 Cor 15:24–26; Rev 20:7–10, 14–15; Rom 16:20.

[43] See Jamie Davies, *The Apocalyptic Paul: Retrospect and Prospect* (Wipf & Stock, 2022).

against the world [God] has made, by which at the same time that world is renewed and reborn."[44]

Paul is an "embattled apostle," as Lisa Bowens has argued, not finally because he is beset by troublesome local opponents in Corinth, undermined by maverick teachers in Galatia, or troubled by the machinations of Roman imperial governance, but because he understands his mission, witness, and service to be part of an apocalyptic contest of cosmic proportions and consequence.[45] We cannot properly grasp "Paul's view of the human being, humanity's place in the cosmos, and how humanity gains access to knowledge of and from God" if we do not acknowledge how these matters are decisively determined by the apocalyptic struggle Paul's gospel envisages and enjoins.[46] This gospel is primarily a gospel of *redemption*, that is, a gospel of the gracious divine rescue of beleaguered and captive creatures out from under the illicit lordship of powers antithetical to both God and human flourishing.[47] As such—and crucially—Paul's gospel witness presents us with a "three-agent drama of salvation" involving God, the human, and the anti-God power that the apostle sometimes provocatively styles "the god of this age" (2 Cor 4:4).[48] Questions of reconciliation, guilt, forgiveness, etc., when they arise are located and understood within this all-encompassing redemptive drama such that justification and the forgiveness of sins represent "a smaller

[44] Donald MacKinnon, "Prayer, Worship, and Life," in *Philosophy and the Burden of Theological Honesty: A Donald MacKinnon Reader*, ed. John C. McDowell (T&T Clark/Continuum, 2011), 59–60.

[45] See Lisa M. Bowens, *An Apostle in Battle: Paul and Spiritual Warfare in 2 Corinthians 12:1–10* (Mohr Siebeck, 2017). Cf. also John Barclay, "Why the Roman Empire was Insignificant to Paul," in *Pauline Churches and Diaspora Jews* (Mohr Siebeck, 2011), 363–87, and Northrop Frye, *The Great Code: The Bible and Literature* (Academic Press Canada, 1981), 164.

[46] Bowens, *Apostle in Battle*, 1.

[47] Paul designates these powers with a range of vocabulary including Satan, the devil, the evil one, the ruler of the power of the air, the god of this age, and Sin and Death and Flesh.

[48] See on this J. Louis Martyn, *Galatians*, AB (Doubleday 1997); "The Gospel Invades Philosophy," in *Paul, Philosophy and the Theopolitical Vision: Critical Engagements with Agamben, Badiou, Zizek and Others*, ed. D. Harink (Wipf and Stock, 2010), 13–36; and "Epilogue: An Essay in Pauline Meta-ethics," in *Divine and Human Agency in Paul and His Cultural Environment*, ed. J. Barclay and S. Gathercole (T&T Clark, 2008), 173–83.

concentric circle within the greater whole of cosmic redemption, of world renewal."[49]

Now, if Christian dogmatics is led to think again about salvation and to reconsider the priority and logic of redemption under pressure from such a fresh hearing of Paul and his gospel, then it will need—among other things—to take explicit theological responsibility for the "third agent" in the three-agent drama: i.e., for the figured cosmic power(s) antithetical to God. Just what can and must be said theologically about *this* enemy? What can and must be said about that *from which* or *from whom* we are delivered? Some may think this "third agent" represents the "third rail" of apocalyptic theology, as it were: a topic too hazardous (even deadly) to handle, at best mythic, at worst mystifying, and so one best left untouched. Yet, as Declan Kelly observes, advocates of a "three-agent soteriology" wager on the contrary that "far from distracting us from reality, the apocalyptic idiom is indispensable for a proper grasp of our drastic situation and its divinely accomplished transformation."[50] Grappling with the devil as a theme in theology is part of weighing up that high-stakes wager. It is also a necessity for any theology which counts Paul's apocalyptic gospel among its mainsprings.

Motivations from Karl Barth

Finally, one might admit another, specifically theological, motivation here, and that is the fascinating treatment of aspects of our theme in the work of the Swiss Reformed theologian Karl Barth under the overarching rubric of *das Nichtige*, or "nothingness." In the context of the doctrine of providence in the *Church Dogmatics* Barth ventures a "clear and short look at demonology," the brevity of which is in inverse proportion to its depth of provocation.[51] In a recorded conversation with students he once summarized his main claims this way:

> There is no fall of angels! I do not deny the existence of the bad [devils] but they are hypostases of *das Nichtige*. God did not create demons. Sin and demons are "impossible possibilities"! They exist

[49] James Kallas, *The Significance of the Synoptic Miracles* (SPCK, 1961), 87. I myself have developed this claim theologically in *Militant Grace: The Apocalyptic Turn and the Future of Christian Theology* (Baker Academic, 2018), 53–70.

[50] Declan Kelly, *The Defeat of Satan: Karl Barth's Three-Agent Account of Salvation* (T&T Clark, 2022), 144–45. I concur; see Ziegler, *Militant Grace*, 28.

[51] Cf. Karl Barth, *Church Dogmatics* III/3, §51, pp. 519–31.

> in a reality without possibility. . . . Satan and his forces are another kind of being in contrast with God and His angels. . . . Demonic action has no ontology.[52]

To which he adds, no less suggestively: "The demythologization which will really hurt them as required cannot consist in questioning their existence. Theological exorcism must be an act of the unbelief which is grounded in faith."[53] Barth's surprising seriousness and realism here, his paradoxical formulations, his evidently sharp revisions to received thinking, and his puzzling call for "theological exorcism" all suggest there might be many more interesting questions and tasks lurking here for Reformed theology than one might have otherwise imagined. Indeed, one way of tackling our theme would be simply to exposit at length and in detail Barth's own doctrine of *das Nichtige*—nothingness—and the demonology it funds.[54] On this occasion I will go another way, though Barth will inevitably make several brief appearances in the chapters that follow.

CONCLUSION

I hope these few initial remarks might serve to motivate at least some interest in my theme. The chapters that follow are offered as an exercise and experiment in diabology. They aim, as my subtitle suggests, to set forth a "brief theology of the devil." I take Christian theology to be the effort to take disciplined, discursive, and intellectual responsibility for the gospel of God before the God of the gospel for the sake of the integrity of the witness and service of the Christian church in and for the world. In that spirit, what follows is an attempt to inquire

[52] Karl Barth, *Table Talk*, recorded and ed. John D. Godsey, *Scottish Journal of Theology Occasional Papers* 10 (Oliver and Boyd, 1963), 72.

[53] Barth, *Church Dogmatics* III/3, 521. For discussion see Philip G. Ziegler, "The First and Final 'No': The Finality of the Gospel and the Old Enemy," in *The Finality of the Gospel: Karl Barth and the Tasks of Eschatology*, ed. Kaitlyn Dugan and Philip G. Ziegler (Brill, 2022), 193–213.

[54] Barth's account of *das Nichtige* is much discussed in the literature. See representatively Wolf Krötke, *Sin and Nothingness in the Theology of Karl Barth*, ed. and trans. Philip G. Ziegler and Christina-Maria Bammel, Studies in Reformed Theology and History NS 10 (Princeton Theological Seminary, 2005); Matthias D. Wüthrich, *Gott und das Nichtige: Zur Rede vom Nichtigen ausgehend von Karl Barths KD §50* (Theologischer Verlag, 2006); and Kelly, *Defeat of Satan*. I have also ventured an essay-length account of Barth's handling of the devil in Ziegler, "First and Final 'No.'"

into—and to assume renewed theological responsibility for—the devil as a topic of Christian doctrine.

In his own 1991 Warfield lectures entitled *Creation and Reality*, Michael Welker ventured a work of what he called the "new biblical theology."[55] One of his driving convictions was a judgment that many key biblical and theological concepts

> which once possessed great orienting power, have now been so dulled by multiple accommodations to prevailing habits of thought and specific conceptions of rationality and moral systems that they function only as ciphers. This dulling of fundamental theological concepts is fatal not only to religious existence and the churches. It also robs cultures and societies of fundamental sources of orientation and important possibilities for self-criticism.[56]

When we revisit theological concepts whose meaning and significance have been blunted over time, we do so in the hope they might help to "impel us to a new and clearer knowledge of God and self . . . in our time and our world."[57] I would like to align the project I undertake here in this book with Welker's vision of just such a "new biblical theology." In what follows, I propose to approach the figure of the devil in an effort to resharpen this particular theological concept for precisely the sorts of reasons Welker avers. I aim to expose afresh our settled—and perhaps stale—received doctrine of the devil to the dramatic and narrative scriptural testimony from which it ultimately derives and to whose force and form it needs finally to do justice. A renewed account of the devil should serve to help check the disorientation and manifold irresponsibility which all too readily fills the vacuum left by silence about this theme. We may expect it also to afford some new and valuable—if backhanded—purchase on the gospel of God and its salutary bearing upon our present life and thought.[58]

55 Michael Welker, *Creation and Reality* (Fortress, 1999), 3–5.

56 Welker, *Creation and Reality*, 4.

57 Welker, *Creation and Reality*, 5.

58 One thinks of Luke 11:24–26: "When the unclean spirit has gone out of a person, it wanders through waterless regions looking for a resting place, but not finding any it says, 'I will return to my house from which I came.' When it returns, it finds it swept and put in order. Then it goes and brings seven other spirits more evil than itself, and they enter and live there, and the last state of that person is worse than the first."

To these ends and in this hope, the argument of the book will unfold as follows. The next chapter will offer an historical sketch of received approaches to the devil in the tradition of Christian doctrine in the West generally, and Reformed theology in particular. It will consider the default dogmatic architecture of diabology and reflect upon the surrounding doctrines which position, shape, and constrain its treatment. These, it turns out, have almost exclusively been the doctrines of the "first article," i.e., doctrines of creation, providence, and within these also angelology. Having traced the mainline of these developments, I will then suggest that there is a fruitful alternative—a "minority report," so to say—to be discerned. I will ally myself with this minority view, advocating for it and elaborating it throughout the chapters that follow. This will involve repositioning the devil doctrinally and in so doing also taking another quite different approach to the matter.

Thereafter, chapters 3, 4, and 5 will trial just such an approach, venturing a biblical-theological exploration of the identity, ontology, and agency of the devil. They are the material heart of the book. These chapters proceed by way of exegetical reflections upon key New Testament materials able to fund renewed thinking about the "devil and all his works" in immediate contact with christological and soteriological concerns. My theological intuition here is that the devil becomes most salient and discernible when in the closest contact with the person and work of the Savior. At a minimum this is a meaningful textual phenomenon; at a maximum, it is an important claim about the very nature of these things. Fixing our attention upon the figure of the devil in a soteriological context will confront us directly with what the devil *does* and only indirectly with what the devil might *be*. This is, as I hope to convince you, just as it should be. Treating diabolical temptation, demonic possession, and devilish falsehood in turn, each of these central chapters will also reflect briefly upon what faithful resistance to—and active disbelief of—these three aspects of the devil's business might mean for the shape of a Christian life.

The final chapter of the book looks to distill and synthesize the diabological insights won across the piece in order finally to give an account of the place of the devil in our doctrine, and briefly to formulate some of the questions and themes that I consider should be at the heart of a Reformed "doctrine of the devil" today.

I hope that, as the argument unfolds across these pages, I will be able to honor the specific mandate of the Annie Kinkead Warfield Lectureship by dealing—as stipulated by the terms of the legacy—with something of "the biblical basis," "the historical development," and "the systematic formulation" of this neglected doctrine in the fresh exposition offered here.[59] I hope too that features of this experiment in diabology will connect—perhaps in surprising and unexpected ways—with the kinds of concerns and questions with which readers themselves are preoccupied. Finally, I hope that thinking theologically about the nature and role of the devil, "God's Adversary and Ours," might also prove properly edifying in one way or another.

[59] Again, to quote from the correspondence of the seminary's "Administrative Committee," 1957, concerning the stipulated terms of the endowment from the Warfield estate.

2
THE DEVIL'S THEOLOGICAL CAREER

> We should establish a religion's degree of truth according to what it makes of the Devil: the more eminent the rank it accords him, the more it testifies that it is concerned with reality, it rejects deceit and lies, that it is serious, that it sets more store by verification than by distraction and consolation.[1]
>
> E. M. Cioran

The first introductory chapter attempted to motivate a new and lively interest in the devil, as it were. I emphasized how aspects of the tradition of Reformed theology pose distinctive challenges to this attempt. To offset these, I briefly canvassed a range of factors—cultural, ecumenical, biblical, and theological—which might motivate theology generally, and Reformed theology in particular, to reconsider the question of the devil with new animus and seriousness. I concluded by recommending an experiment in diabology whose ambition would be to assume theological responsibility for the "third agent," the anti-god power—in short, the devil—in the context of a renewed hearing of the gospel of our redemption today.

[1] Emil M. Cioran, *The Trouble with Being Born*, trans. Richard Howard (Arcade, 1976), 205.

To begin that experiment in earnest, I would like in this chapter to reflect upon certain aspects of the doctrinal handling of the devil in the history of the Western Christian theological tradition. The story is necessarily selective—not least in its interest in observing the fate of the theme up and onto specifically Reformed terrain—though I hope not tendentious. In it, I concentrate upon the dogmatic location of the devil as well as the doctrines which have chiefly served to position, shape, and delimit its treatment. My principal aim is to observe how in the main the doctrine has long been expounded in curious isolation from christological and soteriological reflection. The upshot is the development over time of an increasingly stereotypical and sterile treatment whose growing unimportance finally invites its dissolution. In this story as I shall tell it, Schleiermacher will appear in the role of executioner. However, there are intimations along the way of another possibility. That possibility involves drawing the question of the devil back into close contact with Christology and soteriology. If it were to be recovered and pursued, this alternate path might open up another, brighter future for the devil in Christian dogmatics. The experiment in diabology undertaken in these pages specifically looks to step out into *that* future, and so before this chapter concludes, something more will have to be said about the shape of the constructive argument to come.

POSITIONING THE DEVIL—ANGELS, PRIVATION, AND PROVIDENCE

Already in the second century, Origen of Alexandria—perhaps "the first systematic theologian" of the Christian tradition—asserted programmatically that "No one will be able to know the origin of evils who has not grasped the truth about the so-called devil and his angels, and who he was before he became a devil, and how he became a devil, and what caused his so-called angels to rebel with him."[2] The

[2] Origen, *Against Celsus* 4.65, trans. Henry Chadwick (Cambridge University Press, 1965), 236–37. This characterization of Origen comes from Hugh T. Kerr, *The First Systematic Theologian: Origen of Alexandria* (Princeton Theological Seminary, 1958). The identification of the devil as a fallen angel is pioneered also by Tatian, Justin Martyr, Tertullian, and others; see Jeffrey Burton Russell, *Satan: The Early Christian Tradition* (Cornell University Press, 1981), 30–106. Cf. also Leo I, letter of 447 CE, which makes the standard claims about privative insubstantial evil and angelic fall; see the text of the letter in Heinrich Denzinger, *Enchiridion Symbolorum: Compendium*

early Christian tradition largely owned this as an axiom. Such preoccupation with the origin and nature of the devil as a fallen angel is both enduring and widespread in early Christianity.[3] As Gabrielle Thomas has argued, while its role in the business of theodicy may be unsteady, the construal of the devil as an angel now turned into "an enemy of God and humankind" reaches into the late fourth century and remains a defining mark of the influential and sophisticated diabology of the Cappadocians.[4]

Arguably, the theological career of the devil in the West, however, begins in earnest sometime later in Augustine's work. For, as Irena Backus observes, it was Augustine who first offered a "systematized demonology" incorporating a distinctive account of the devil that "provided the source for all subsequent theories" up to and as late as the eighteenth century.[5] This was not because the devil was an overwhelming preoccupation for Augustine, but rather because of the way his questions and their answers come to shape so much of what follows. Of course, this is true as a rule of Augustine's wider influence upon much later Christian doctrine; but if that is so then the case of the devil is certainly no exception. Haunted by the ghost of Manichaeism, Augustine is particularly sharp in resisting anything

---

of Creeds, Definitions, and Declarations on Matters of Faith and Morals, 43rd ed., ed. Peter Hunermann (Ignatius, 2012), §286. Interesting here is Alan McGill's view that "Patristic zeal to counteract a model of Satan as a demiurge may have, as a secondary effect, perpetuated misplaced certainty about the existence of Satan as a creature, an angel, and hence, a person." Alan McGill, "A Truth Best Told Through Fiction: On Developing the Catholic Presentation of the Doctrine of Satan as a Mythic Probe into the Possible" (PhD diss., University of Birmingham, 2015), 152.

3 See Henry Ansgar Kelly, *Satan: A Biography* (Cambridge University Press, 2006), esp. ch. 9, "Lucifer and the New Biography of Satan," 191–214. For a wider survey of patristic sources on this theme see Russell, *Satan*.

4 See Gabrielle Thomas, "Basil of Caesarea and Gregory of Nazianzus on the Role of the Devil in Problems of Evil and Suffering," *International Journal of Systematic Theology* 26, no. 4 (2024): 364–66.

5 Irena Backus, "Demons," in *The Oxford Guide to the Historical Reception of Augustine*, ed. Karla Pollmann and Willemien Otten (Oxford University Press, 2013), 867 (867–70). Of course, Western Christian theology was haunted by the specter of Manichaeism and its derivatives for centuries after Augustine in the figures of the Bogomils, Cathars, etc., on the margins of orthodoxy and beyond. See Steven Runciman, *The Medieval Manichee: A Study of the Christian Dualist Heresy* (Cambridge University Press, 1947) and more recently Yuri Stoyanov, *The Other God: Dualist Religions from Antiquity to the Cathar Heresy* (Yale University Press, 2000).

that might encourage "dualism" in Christian doctrine. Three key teachings secure this point time and again: first, the identification of the devil as an angel, and so as one of God's good *creatures*; second, the characterization of evil as *privation*; and third, the firm coordinating of the devil's will to the outworking of divine providence. These same three interlocking claims prove abidingly decisive in shaping diabology in the West.[6]

A first and decisive feature of Augustine's treatment is that it asks and answers the question of the devil within the context of the doctrine of creation generally, and—in keeping with Origen's suggestion—of angelology in particular.[7] As all creaturely being comes from God who is supremely good, creaturely being itself simply is good, though derivatively and mutably so. The devil, too, is a creature whose nature *qua* creature is and remains inalienably good. As an *angelic* creature, the devil is a "rational or intellectual" entity of a purely spiritual kind, i.e., without a material body or any of its attendant sensations and appetites. As such, like all angels, the devil acts without impediment and reasons nondiscursively, i.e., without processes of induction, deduction, or discovery but by rather an immediate perception of the essences of things. These determinations of the devil as *creature* and as *angel* prove crucial to much else that follows.

The second key feature of Augustine's treatment of the devil is its framing by the conception of evil as a *privation* of good.[8] As God's creation, all of nature is good simply by virtue of being. As the antithesis of good, evil cannot share in being, it cannot be. "Evil has no positive nature," Augustine explains, but is insubstantial, without being in its own right. It "is," rather, only the depletion and deprivation of

[6] Russell, *Satan*, 195–96, also suggests that Augustine "synthesized existing diabology, and, adding new insights, constructed a relatively coherent approach to the problem of evil" of lasting influence. Cf. also the final chapters of Neil Forsyth, *The Old Enemy: Satan & the Combat Myth* (Princeton University Press, 1987), 387–440, where Augustine's teaching and its transformation of the theme are insightfully discussed.

[7] See Augustine, *City of God* 11.29, 32, 33; 12.1–9, 25. All quotations taken from Augustine, *The City of God Against the Pagans*, ed. and trans. R. W. Dyson (Cambridge University Press, 1998).

[8] See Augustine, *The Enchiridion on Faith, Hope and Charity* 4, trans. Boniface Ramsey (New City, 1999); and *On the Nature of the Good Against the Manichees* §4, in *Augustine: Earlier Writings*, ed. and trans. John H. S. Burleigh (Westminster Press, 1953), 327.

being, the corruption of creaturely good. In itself, evil is *nothing*. This is, of course, not to deny the fact of evil in the world but rather to specify its peculiar metaphysical quality. On such an account, "there can never be things which are wholly evil" because, "being nothing in itself," evil must "reside" or "be an aspect of some actual entity."[9] Grammatically, evil is only ever predicate, never subject. If this is so, then the devil cannot be thought to be essentially or entirely evil, for there can be no such thing: corruption which consumed the entire good of a creature would consume the thing itself and thereby cease to be. Thus "nothing evil exists *in itself*," not even the devil; to admit otherwise would be a metaphysical nonsense, would call into question the goodness of the Creator, and would constitute a retreat into just the Manichaean dualism Augustine himself had once embraced, found wanting, and then vigorously resisted.[10]

Taken together, these two key features—angelic creaturely being and privative, corrupting evil—fund the characterization of the devil as *fallen*. The understanding receives biblical impulse from texts like Jude 1:6 ("And the angels who did not keep their own position but deserted their proper dwelling, he has kept in eternal chains in deepest darkness for the judgment of the great Day."), Luke 10:18 ("[Jesus] said to them, 'I watched Satan fall from heaven like a flash of lightning.'"), and 2 Peter 2:4 ("For if God did not spare the angels when they sinned but cast them into hell and committed them to chains of deepest darkness to be kept until the judgment").[11] What is true of fallen angels generally is true of the devil in particular, and superlatively so: the "evil angels also were not constituted evil by God, but were made evil by sinning."[12] Thus, for Augustine, the subject matter of diabology is precisely that particular angel who became the devil when he "first rose in rebellion with his impious company."[13]

[9] Augustine, *City of God* 12.3; *Enchiridion* 4.13.

[10] Augustine, *Enchiridion* 4.13. Augustine's *On the Nature of the Good*, 324–48, culminates in several lengthy chapters (41–48) decrying the absurdities and errors of the Manichaeans. For discussion see J. Kevin Coyle, *Manichaeism and Its Legacy* (Brill, 2009), esp. ch. 16, "God's Place in Augustine's Anti-Manichaean Polemic," 265–82.

[11] Augustine, *City of God* 11.33, cites 2 Pet 2:4 directly as its rationale for the division of angels into two "companies," good and bad.

[12] Augustine, *On the Nature of the Good* 33.

[13] Augustine, *Enchiridion* 9.28.

Again, these same two features of Augustine's account—the creaturely goodness of angels and the privative dynamic of evil—together dictate that the fall of the devil can have no natural cause: if we ask why the devil fell, we cannot point to any cause seated in the devil's angelic nature or being. Rather, the fall is ascribed purely to a "deficient" will. The devil's corruption is "caused" by an evil will which itself has no cause: for "the first evil will is that which was made evil by no other."[14] It is, in short, "voluntary," spontaneous, and in no way necessary. Neither do the inferior objects of disordered desire nor the downward pull of bodily appetites corrupt the angelic will, because as pure spiritual substance it is hampered by none of them. No, the angelic will "makes itself evil" by its very willing. Here is but a willful "turning away" from God and "toward itself," a movement of "pride." The upshot is that the devil stands firmly, if first, in the ranks of all "God's enemies"—whether angelic or human—who "are so called in the Scriptures not by nature, but because they oppose His authority by their vice."[15] Nothing in good creation opposes God because of what it *is*, the devil included.

The third key feature of Augustine's account of the devil is its firm superintendence by divine providence. "However strong the wills either of angels or of [human beings], whether good or evil, whether they will what God wills, or will something else," Augustine explains, "the will of the Omnipotent is always undefeated."[16] The devil, too, is encompassed by sovereign divine providence: his evil willing and doing in no way impedes its course. Rather, like all creaturely willing and doing, that of the captain of the fallen angels is also bound to serve the accomplishment of the divine will, its very evil made to serve—albeit "strangely" and "ineffably"—divine mercy in the working out of salvation and divine punishment in the execution of justice.[17] Augustine takes the "binding" of the devil described in the Book of Revelation (Rev 20:1–3) as a dramatic depiction of this same truth: namely, that diabolical rebellion is constrained and

[14] Augustine, *City of God* 12.6. Other citations in this paragraph from the same book and chapter.

[15] Augustine, *City of God* 12.3.

[16] Augustine, *Enchiridion* 26.102.

[17] Augustine, *Enchiridion* 26.100. Cf. *City of God* 14.27.

runs its course only within the firm channels of divine permission and providence.[18]

In sum, Augustine positions the figure of the devil dogmatically at the intersection of claims about the goodness of creation, the nature of angelic being and willing, the privative quality of evil, and the exercise of meticulous divine providence.[19] The identity, ontology, and agency of the devil are decisively determined by the conjunction of just these themes. In this way what is said theologically about the devil is almost entirely confined to what we might call "the first article" of the creed. The devil makes no notable appearance and plays no substantive role in the lengthy history of salvation that makes up the bulk of Augustine's *City of God*. And while some late sermons of the bishop of Carthage do memorably cast the cross as a "mousetrap" laid to catch the devil, their rhetoric reflects the instrumental idiom of providence more than it signals any developed theory of redemption.[20]

Now, this distinctive doctrinal conjunction continues to configure the handling of the devil in the centuries after Augustine. We find the same claims and arguments rehearsed and elaborated in a chain of influential texts that run up through the center of the Medieval tradition in the West. From Pseudo-Dionysius's *Divine Names*, through Peter Lombard's *Sentences*, Anselm's *On the Fall of the Devil*, and on to the *Summa Theologica* of Thomas Aquinas and his extensive tract *On Evil* (*De malo*), angelology, privative evil, and divine providence

[18] Augustine, *City of God* 20.8.

[19] Reassuringly, the main thesis of Gregory Wiebe's recent and extensive study of Augustine's demonology confirms that for Augustine "demons emerge as a highly integrated component of his broader theology, rooted in his conception of angels as the ministers of all creation under God, and informed by the doctrine of evil as privation and his understanding of the fall, his thoughts on human embodiment, desire, visions, and the limits of human knowledge . . ." Gregory D. Wiebe, *Fallen Angels in the Theology of St. Augustine* (Oxford University Press, 2021), 4.

[20] On this see the detailed discussion of the texts by David Scott-Macnab, "Augustine's Trope of the Crucifixion as a Trap for the Devil and Its Survival in the English Middle Ages," *Viator* 46, no. 3 (2015): 1–20. Books 4 and 13 of Augustine's *De Trinitate* include a concise characterization of the devil as an angel of darkness masquerading as an angel of light, a "false mediator of death," a prideful "lover of power," and "assailant of justice," in a somewhat more immediately soteriological context. See Augustine, *The Trinity*, ed. and trans. Edmund Hill, OP (New City, 1991), 4.13–20; 13.16–23; as well as 15.34, 44.

continue to work together to fix and define the devil doctrinally.[21] The continuity of this tradition is explicitly manifest in the fact that citations from Augustine and Dionysius regularly provide *sed contra* propositions and authoritatively inform the replies to stated objections in Thomas's formal arguments on the theme.

Downstream from Augustine and firmly within his wake, theologians from across this long period continue to teach that the devil has an angelic nature, created and so good, being immaterial, spiritual, and "intellectual" in substance and power. The fall of the devil has will and not nature at its root: it is not coincident with his creation nor does anything external cause it; the evil lies in the spontaneous willing itself which (in keeping with the privative character of evil) depletes, deprives, and corrupts the form and virtues of angelic being without destroying it. Despite arising from malice against God and creatures, the activity of the devil, as Thomas remarks, ever remains part of the ministry of angels, for God "knows how to make orderly use of evil by ordering it to good."[22] Providential superintendence everywhere constrains high-creaturely evil, securing at once the futility but also the ultimate utility of the angelic rebellion in the unfolding of God's mysterious ways.

Such medieval reiterations bring scholastic refinements, to be sure. Especially in the work of Thomas, new precision is won. Three examples must suffice. First, we learn from Thomas that the devil falls because he willed to be like God, desiring to grasp prematurely what he would have attained had he remained steadfast: the fault lies not in what he desired (i.e., to be like God) but in the way in which

[21] Pseudo-Dionysius, *The Divine Names* 4.18–35, in *The Complete Works of Pseudo-Dionysius*, trans. Colm Luibheid (Paulist, 1987); Peter Lombard, *Sentences*, bk. 2, *On Creation*, trans. Giulio Silano (PIMS, 2008); Anselm, *On the Fall of the Devil*, in *The Complete Treatises*, ed. and trans. Thomas Williams (Hackett, 2022), 177–22; Thomas Aquinas, *On Evil*, trans. Richard Regan, ed. Brian Davies (Oxford University Press, 2003), esp. q. 16; Thomas Aquinas, *Summa Theologica* I, trans. Fathers of the English Dominican Province (Burns, Oates and Washbourne, 1927), qq. 48, 50–64, 114 (esp. 48, 63, 64, 114). Also notable is the fact that Canon 1 of Lateran IV (1215) secures the teaching of the devil as a fallen angel as Church dogma: "The devil and the other demons were indeed created by God good by nature but they became bad through themselves; man, however, sinned at the suggestion of the devil" (Denzinger, *Enchiridion Symbolorum*, §800). The same teaching is essentially distilled for the East in John of Damascus, *On the Orthodox Faith*, 2.4, 10, 27; 4.20.

[22] Thomas Aquinas, *Summa Theologica* I, q. 144, art. 1.

he desired it (i.e., immediately by his own striving and not in due course by grace).[23] Second, Thomas secures the received teaching that the fall of the devil is *irrevocable*, and does so specifically as an implication of the nature and dynamics of angelic being and willing: precisely *qua* fallen *angel* is the devil irredeemable.[24] Third, Thomas teaches that the devil's doings are *natural* in a quite specific sense. As he explains, the devil and demons "can do the same things that good angels can, since both have the same nature" despite differences "according to the goodness or wickedness of the will."[25] One upshot of this is that, as he goes on to explain, "in the strict sense, the demons cannot work miracles, nor can any creature, but God alone: since in the strict sense a miracle is something done outside the order of the entire created nature, under which order every power of a creature is contained."[26] The devil does no miracles, only "wonders."[27] Despite popular usage and the intuitions which fund it, the evil associated with the devil is not in fact *supernatural* in the strict sense. It is, rather, "natural" precisely in the specific sense that it expresses the movements of the fallen will of a *created* angelic being.[28] The devil is a creature, and his actions however distorted by evil are themselves never more than creaturely.

23 Thomas Aquinas, *On Evil* 16.3. Cf. Anselm, *On the Fall of the Devil* 4.

24 Thomas Aquinas, *On Evil* 16.5. A point also secured by Anselm, *On the Fall of the Devil* 17. The argument is very subtle, and not perhaps fully persuasive.

25 Thomas Aquinas, *On Evil* 16.12.

26 Thomas Aquinas, *Summa Theologica* I, q. 144, art. 4. Here, too, Thomas refines a pattern that reaches back into the early Christian centuries; cf. Tertullian, *Apology* 8, trans. T. Herbert Bindley (Parker and Co, 1890): "Every spirit is winged; so it is with angels, so it is with demons. Thus in a moment they are everywhere; all the world is to them one spot; what is being done, and where, it is as easy for them to know as to tell. Their swiftness passes for divinity, because their real nature is unknown."

27 The devil can perform a "*mirum* but not *miraculum*." On this see Stuart Clark, *Thinking with Demons: The Idea of Witchcraft in Early Modern Europe* (Oxford University Press, 1999), esp. ch. 11, "The Devil in Nature," 161–78, for the early modern reception and confirmation of this claim.

28 Thomas Aquinas, *On Evil* 16.6: "The devil does everything evilly regarding what he does by free choice. But properly speaking, his natural actions are good, since those natural actions are from God, who established their nature." Devilish action as creaturely action is always at once good and evil in this sense. While quite a fine point, it actually bears importantly on the understanding of the moral force of temptation: humans are morally culpable for sin since devilish temptation is not an irresistible supernatural force, but a natural (if powerful) one that can be resisted naturally.

Importantly, in all this, the dogmatic placement of the devil in the "first article of the creed" is confirmed time and again in the central line of tradition. Thomas's placement of the matter in the *prima pars* of the *Summa* ensures the question of the devil remains chiefly a matter of the doctrine of creation, of good natures and privative evil, of angelic being and willing, and of providential divine government. All the most important decisions about the being and doing of the devil are taken here within these specific doctrinal coordinates. As we have seen, presuppositions supplied by angelology prove to be particularly decisive: that and how we have conceived of the devil as a personal agent, intelligent and volitional, enacting intentions, preternatural (but *not* supernatural) in power, all trade upon them. The question of the devil is asked and answered entirely within their scope. All this proves hugely influential for subsequent Catholic and Protestant theologies alike. So, too, is the very *way* the question is asked and answered in the scholastic *quaestio* format. Even long after the medieval *quaestio* format itself is left off, this set of traditional questions and their received answers continue to set what we might call the "agenda of diabology."

There is a curious discrepancy in all this. In the main, where the biblical witness is most vociferous about the devil—namely, in the gospel witness to the outworking of salvation in Christ—the theological tradition is rather reticent. And where the theological tradition speaks and thinks most about the devil—namely, in the context of its exposition and elaboration of the first article of the creed—the biblical witness is most reticent. Yet, the tradition worked out from Augustine to Thomas both specifies this firm dogmatic placement of the devil and bequeaths a "canon" of diabolical questions and themes, concepts and convictions which pass into subsequent dogmatic theology.

REFORMED ACCOUNTS—CONTINUITY AND DISSOLUTION

The early-modern Reformed theologians who shaped that tradition between the sixteenth to eighteenth centuries and the confessions they authored received and largely approved of this traditional dogmatic agenda and architecture. Understood as an angelic, spiritual creature who falls away from God in a perverse act of spontaneous willing—"an affectation to divinity"—before the fall of humanity, they affirm that the devil is "unchangeably bad . . . eternally rejected and incurably hardened in evil," able to "do nothing but sin . . . voluntarily [and] successively to eternity."[29] The evil he does is firmly governed by divine providence and done with divine permission. As Calvin has it: "Let it remain fixed that except by God's will and assent [Satan] can do nothing."[30] Keenly refusing dualism, the first article of the creed—i.e., the sphere of the doctrines of creation and providence—remains the chief location of teaching about the devil and reflection upon the theme.[31]

Distinctive Reformed emphases do make themselves felt, to be sure. For example, election now joins divine sovereignty and providence in channeling the devil's fall and subsequent actions: like all creaturely occurrence, the devil's course, too, "rests upon an eternal counsel of God according to which God resolved not to hinder it," for God eternally "decreed to allow [Satan] to fall away."[32] The doctrine of election also gives the devil's unwilled service two distinct appointed ends: as regards the reprobate, the devil is made to serve the ends of divine righteousness and the just punishment of sin; as regards the elect, he serves to "test" and "exercise" them in humility and patience.[33] The Reformed also take an especial interest in the role of the devil in the human fall into sin, now regularly styled "the violation of the covenant of works." Identified traditionally with the serpent in the garden, the devil, it is said, instigates, deceives,

[29] Heinrich Heppe, *Reformed Dogmatics: Set Out and Illustrated from the Sources*, trans. G. T. Thompson (Allen & Unwin, 1950), 216–17.

[30] John Calvin, *Institutes of the Christian Religion*, trans. Ford Lewis Battles (Westminster, 1960), 1.14.17. Echoed in *French Confession*, article 8; *Belgic Confession*, articles 12, 13; *Second Helvetic Confession*, "Of Angels and the Devil"; *Westminster Confession* 5.6, 6.1. Cf. also J. Wollebius, *Compendium Theologiae Christianae* (1626), in John W. Beardslee III, ed., *Reformed Dogmatics* (Baker Book House, 1977), 7.2, "The Governance of Angels," pp. 63–64, which rings all the traditional bells, including placement.

[31] For concise summary discussion see Jan Rohls, *Reformed Confessions: Theology from Zurich to Barmen*, trans. John Hoffmeyer (Westminster John Knox, 1998), 62–64, who stresses the ambition to avoid dualism while also refusing to make God the origin of evil.

[32] Heppe, *Reformed Dogmatics*, 218.

[33] Heppe, *Reformed Dogmatics*, 218. This closely echoes Thomas's teaching noted above.

and tempts the first human pair into disobedience; yet these "docile pupils of Satan" are not thereby excused, because "God had equipped [them] with sufficient strength to overcome the adversary easily."[34] With its amplified interest in the devil's role in the human fall into sin and recourse to the doctrine of election in framing the devil's own fall and fate, Reformed teaching does in this way bring the devil into somewhat closer contact with soteriology, even as it ever more insistently keeps it firmly under the Creator's thumb. Such commitments rhyme best, perhaps, with the depiction of the Satan of the Book of Job: the angelic bad boy of the heavenly court, who despite ill will and the power to deprive the human creature of so much, is still put to use firmly and directly within the designs of God's providence. Indeed, I would suggest that we may take Job's Satan as the paradigmatic figure of the long doctrinal tradition we have been tracing to this point.

Where teaching about the devil persists as an element of positive Reformed doctrine up and into the nineteenth century—and it does not always do so, as we shall see—its treatment continues to respect the received canon of diabology: evidence both Francis Turretin's *Institutes* and Charles Hodge's *Systematic Theology*, the textbooks of Reformed doctrine, taught throughout the Atlantic world (and beyond) right up and into the twentieth century. For all their differences, Turretin and Hodge together affirm the received approach: both treat the devil chiefly (even exhaustively) within their angelology. All the traditional claims—about the "spontaneous," purely volitional quality of the high angel's fall, its deleterious object being an "affectation of equality with God," its irreversibility and permanence, its permissive superintendence by God, etc.—are rehearsed here.[35] Hodge in particular keenly delimits devilish evil and does so, very traditionally, by direct appeal to the nature of angelic creaturehood. Addressing the nature of devils he explains:

> The same limitations, of course, belong to their agency as belong to that of the holy angels. (1) They are dependent on God and can act only under his control and by his permission. (2) Their operations

[34] Heppe, *Reformed Dogmatics*, 301–6, 310–11.

[35] Francis Turretin, *Institutes of Elenctic Theology*, vol. 1, ed. J. T. Dennison Jr., trans. George Musgrave Giger, (P&R Publishing, 1992), 9.5, pp. 601–3.

> must be according to the laws of nature, and (3) They cannot interfere with the freedom and responsibility of men.[36]

Highly unusually—and no doubt under pressure from his strict affirmation of the factuality of biblical testimony—Hodge does not conclude his account before addressing the question of demonic possession, its biblical attestation, and the refutation of objections against its present-day occurrence. Still, the upshot of this excursus is very guarded and deflationary. He observes that, while "we do not deny what is plainly recorded in the Scriptures as fact on this subject," nothing should be referred to devilish agency save it can be positively proven to be such. A high bar indeed.[37]

We might draw from all this that Irena Backus was right: right up into the nineteenth century Augustine continued to serve as the ancient patron of a discourse about the devil which becomes an increasingly stereotyped locus firmly anchored in the doctrines of the first article of the creed. The perdurance of this dogmatic architecture and of the fixed questions and answers which fill it out is consistently and readily visible in textbook accounts well up and into the modern period. Located in this place and handled in this way, the doctrine of the devil in fact does very little dogmatic work. Jeffrey Burton Russell observes that place of the devil in the teaching of the Reformed becomes, as he insightfully puts it, "secure but seldom salient."[38] When toward the end of the nineteenth century Philip Schaff compiled a widely read harmony of Reformed confessional teachings, his comprehensive summary of the substance of received doctrine tellingly required no mention of the devil whatsoever at any point.[39]

Now, this "secure but seldom salient" tradition of first-article diabology meets its comeuppance at the hands of Friedrich Schleiermacher. In his influential treatment of the devil in §§44–45 of *The Christian Faith*, the devil dutifully appears as an "appendix" to his

[36] Charles Hodge, *Systematic Theology*, 3 vols. (1872–73; repr., Eerdmans, 1981), 1:643–48.

[37] Hodge, *Systematic Theology*, 1:647.

[38] Jeffrey Burton Russell, *Mephistopheles: The Devil in the Modern World* (Cornell University Press, 1986), 44.

[39] Philip Schaff, *The Harmony of the Reformed Confessions, as Related to the Present State of Evangelical Theology* (Dodd, Mead & Co, 1877).

doctrine of creation generally, and to his angelology in particular.[40] So far, so traditional. Yet his account dissolves itself by design. "The idea of the Devil as developed among us," he writes, "is so unstable that we cannot expect anyone to be convinced of its truth; but, besides, our Church has never made doctrinal use of the idea."[41] If you thought the devil could serve as either an ultimate explanation of human evil or a device for conceiving of the punishment of sin, you would be wrong. Reformed confessions, Schleiermacher contends, knew better than to invoke "so hazardous an idea" to these ends. Indeed, at best doctrinal claims about the devil require more elucidation than they in turn lend to our understanding of the faith. At worst they are simply theologically incoherent.[42] As Daniel Pedersen has convincingly shown, Schleiermacher rejects received teaching about the devil on grounds of both "internal inconsistency" and its low, even negative yield in explaining the phenomena of evil and human sin.[43]

Yet Schleiermacher's criticism and dismissal of the place of the devil in our doctrine also has a second and explicitly exegetical mainspring. Both here in *The Christian Faith* and in finer detail in his *Life of Jesus*, he contends that the use Jesus and the disciples make of the language of the devil and its cognates as found in the Gospels is entirely incidental to their message of the kingdom of God. Examination of particulars leads him to the view that Christ's preaching involves no specific cogent idea of the devil and offers no new or distinct teaching. Rather, with the "devil" as with other idioms, he explains, "Christ made use of those ideas as did all others at the time, for he always made himself understandable and worked within the ideational framework of the day."[44] In other words: everything said in and with this idiom could be said equally well without it; the devil is of the rhetoric but not the stuff of evangelical teaching,

[40] F. D. E. Schleiermacher, *The Christian Faith*, trans. H. R. Mackintosh (T&T Clark, 1928), section 1, §§44–45, pp. 161–67.

[41] This is the thesis of Schleiermacher, *Christian Faith* §44, p. 161.

[42] For exhaustive discussion of the detailed arguments here see Daniel J. Pedersen, *Schleiermacher's Theology of Sin and Nature: Agency, Value, and Modern Theology* (Routledge, 2020), esp. 17–35.

[43] Pedersen, *Schleiermacher's Theology of Sin and Nature*, 30. Cf. Schleiermacher, *Christian Faith* §45, pp. 163–67.

[44] F. D. E. Schleiermacher, *The Life of Jesus*, ed. Jack C. Verheyden, trans. S. Maclean Gilmour (Fortress, 1975), 320 (the full discussion runs from pp. 309–21).

a feature of the historic communication of the gospel but not of the substance of the gospel itself. The devil—being accidental and adiaphorous in this way—has no integral place in the Redeemer's own God-consciousness as we encounter it in the Gospels and so it can and ought not to be enjoined upon the doctrine and piety of the body of Christian believers. So, Schleiermacher famously concludes:

> Since that from which we are to be redeemed remains the same (as does also the manner of our redemption) whether there be a devil or no, the question as to his existence is not one for Christian theology but for cosmology, in the widest sense of that word. It is exactly similar to questions as to the nature of the firmament and the heavenly bodies. In Christian dogmatics we have nothing either to affirm or deny on such subjects; and similarly we are just as little concerned to dispute the concept of the devil as to establish it.[45]

We might think of Schleiermacher's judgment as culminating the logic of the devil's firm dogmatic positioning within the first article of the creed. So complete is it here that the remainder of our doctrine—and most especially our soteriology—is entirely quarantined from it. Here, the place of the devil in our doctrine proves finally to be neither salient nor secure. The reticence of modern theology—Reformed or otherwise—regarding the devil finds an outstanding exemplar and encouragement in Schleiermacher's case against its dogmatic coherence and exegetical necessity. He gives a rigorously argued account of a common intuition that the devil is a feature of a passé worldview, part of the ancient mythical husk that needs to be shucked in any modern effort to access the kernel of the gospel.[46]

[45] Schleiermacher, *Christian Faith* §45, p. 167.

[46] Explicit echoes of Schleiermacher's approach, arguments, and judgments resound after him. See Julius Wilhelm Kaftan, *Dogmatik*, 7th and 8th expanded ed. (Mohr, 1920), 368–70: "A doctrine cannot be established concerning Satan any more than concerning angels, since faith has nothing to say about it and the dogmatic explanation of evil gains nothing by it" (p. 370, my translation); and the 2nd rev. ed. of Theodore Haering, *The Christian Faith: A System of Dogmatics*, trans. John Dickie and George Ferries, vol. 1 (Hodder & Stoughton, 1915), 481–87: "For Dogmatics, no further light is shed upon the aspect of the great problem [of sin] which has brought us to the conclusion last discussed, by the Biblical idea of the Evil One" (p. 481).

THE DOGMATIC LEGACY—A MINORITY REPORT?

Could there be another different future for the devil in our doctrine beside this sad Berlin denouement? Yes, I think there is.

One way to catch sight of it is to extend the story of this dogmatic history just a little further beyond Schleiermacher to Karl Barth. If we do so, what do we find? In one sense Barth keeps faith with the tradition we have been tracing. His discussion of the devil appears within his treatment of the doctrine of creation in the third volume of the *Church Dogmatics*, and therein within his discussion of divine providence, and furthermore within that, as an appendix to his angelology. By assigning the devil this dogmatic location, Barth receives and repeats the form of the great tradition as we have seen. Yet, into that very traditional form and location Barth inserts a quite disruptive material claim. Arguably, his most important definition of the "nothingness" figured by the devil is also his most concise: "The true nothingness is that which brought Jesus Christ to the cross, and that which He defeated there."[47] Barth's definition here is entirely soteriological in substance, riveting theological understanding of the devil first and foremost to Christ and his victorious work upon the cross. If one follows Barth's material claim rather than the form of his dogmatic architecture, we are led to consider whether the truth about the devil should actually be sought not within the scope of the first article of the creed, but within its second article, i.e., within theological reflection upon the dramatic outworking of salvation in Christ.[48] Upon such an axiomatic claim as this one might hang a very different diabology indeed.

[47] Karl Barth, *Church Dogmatics* III/3, 305.

[48] The ambiguity or tension between form and content here is, of course, softened somewhat when one recalls that Barth's doctrine of creation is itself already christologically and soteriologically inflected in virtue of being ordered to covenant and so to salvation, i.e., in virtue of creation itself being construed from the first as but the "outer basis of the covenant of salvation." On the complexities of Barth's account of nothingness in this regard see both Matthias D. Wüthrich, "An Entirely Different Theodicy: Karl Barth's Interpretation of Human Suffering in the Context of his Doctrine of *das Nichtige*," *International Journal of Systematic Theology* 23, no. 4 (2021): 593–616, as well as Günter Thomas, "Sin and Evil," in *The Oxford Handbook of Karl Barth*, ed. Paul Dafydd Jones and Paul T. Nimmo (Oxford University Press, 2019), 354–72. Cf. also my essay, "The First and Final 'No': The Finality of the Gospel and the Old Enemy," in *The Finality of the Gospel: Karl Barth and the Tasks of Eschatology*, ed. Kaitlyn Dugan and Philip G. Ziegler (Brill, 2022), 193–213.

And Barth is not alone in signaling the possibility of another, better path along which diabology might be pursued. The suggestion just espied in his work is one already there to be seen lurking in earlier stages of the Reformed tradition. We can already catch sight of it in, for example, the way the devil is handled by Calvin's *French Catechism* and in the *Heidelberg Confession*. Notably, such catechetical writings sit more lightly upon received dogmatic architecture and are by their nature more closely and directly exposed to biblical language and forms. Both these texts securely intimate that the devil is in fact supremely salient to orderly reflection on the heart of the Christian gospel of salvation and its entailments.

We begin by calling to mind the famous opening question and answer of the *Heidelberg Catechism*, which asks "What is your only comfort in life and in death?" and replies in part: "That I, with body and soul, both in life and in death, am not my own, but belong to my faithful Savior Jesus Christ, who with His precious blood has fully satisfied for all my sins, and redeemed me from all the power of the devil . . ."[49] Notable is the summary presentation of the saving work of Christ as a work of *redemption*, redemption out from under "the power of the devil." The work of atonement which Christ effects by his death on the cross is a satisfaction for sin, to be sure, but it is always also deliverance. In fact, the latter is arguably one of the *Catechism*'s controlling soteriological images: asked later why they call Jesus Christ "Our Lord" in the Apostles' Creed, the faithful student replies: "Because, not with gold or silver, but with His precious blood, He has redeemed and purchased us, body and soul, from sin and from all the power of the devil, to be His own."[50] Sin and "the power of the devil" are now set in apposition to one another, two designations for the antithetical power from which the Christian is set free by the costly exercise of Christ's lordship. Liberation from the "power of the devil" is, of course, the logical inverse of the *Catechism*'s repeated and positive emphasis on the Christian as one who *belongs* to Christ. This is emphasized once again in the gloss given to

[49] *Heidelberg Catechism* Q1. There is a valuable trilingual edition of the text: *The Heidelberg Catechism in German, Latin, and English* (Charles Scribner, 1863).

[50] *Heidelberg Catechism* Q34. The Latin version, the *Catechesis Palatina*, renders Q34 thus: "Quia corpus et animam nostram a peccatis, non auro, nec argento, sed pretioso suo sanguine redimens, *et ab omni potestate Diaboli liberans* nos sibi proprios vidicavit" (emphasis added).

the second petition of the Lord's Prayer: "'Your kingdom come,' that is: So govern us by Your Word and Spirit, that we submit ourselves to you always more and more; preserve and increase Your Church; destroy the works of the devil, every power that exalts itself against you, and all wicked devices formed against Your Holy Word, until the fullness of Your Kingdom come, wherein You shall be all in all."[51]

Calvin's first *French Catechism* of 1537/38 displays all these same sensibilities. Asked about the nature of Christ's work of salvation, the Genevan catechumen answers: "Though our iniquity should deserve something quite different, this merciful Father yet, according to his unspeakable benignity, shows himself . . . [and] recalls us from error to the right way, from death to life, from ruin to salvation, from the kingdom of the devil to his own reign."[52] And here again the force of the second petition of the Lord's Prayer is to desire the kingdom "finally be perfect and accomplished, that is to say, in the revelation of his judgment, in which day he alone will be extolled and will be all things in all people after having gathered and received his own in glory and having demolished and completely overthrown the reign of Satan."[53] The saving work of Christ and the exercise of his dominion having been cast explicitly as a redemption from the antithetical power of the devil, the same conception is then further extended in characterizing the Christian life. To "fight against sin and the devil in this life with a free conscience" *just is* the reason why one is called a Christian, according to the *Heidelberg Catechism*.[54] To be protected, sanctified, and ruled by God's grace *just is* "to be freed from the evil one," Calvin explains.[55] To this Calvin adds in the *Institutes*:

> The fact that the devil is everywhere called God's adversary and ours ought to fire us to an unceasing struggle against him . . . If we are minded to affirm Christ's Kingdom as we ought, we must wage irreconcilable war with him who is plotting its ruin.[56]

51 *Heidelberg Catechism* Q123.

52 *Calvin's Catechism* (1537), in James T. Dennison, ed., *Reformed Confessions of the 16th and 17th Centuries in English Translation*, 4 vols. (Reformation Heritage Books, 2008–14), 1:358.

53 *Calvin's Catechism* (1537) Q24, in Dennison, *Reformed Confessions*, 1:382.

54 *Heidelberg Catechism* Q32.

55 *Calvin's Catechism* (1537) Q24, in Dennison, *Reformed Confessions*, 1:384.

56 Calvin, *Institutes* (1559) 1.14.15.

To be schooled in the faith by these Reformed instruments is to meet the devil first and foremost as one from whom we are freed by Christ, one against whom we ourselves contend in Christ, and one whose final overthrow is the substance of what we hope from Christ. Notable in all these instances is how the conception of redemption is fundamentally agonistic and martial rather than transactional. Tropes of *victory* rather than ransom fill out the vision; the fundamental dynamic of the situation is militantly oppositional. "To the extent that Christ's kingdom is upbuilt, Satan with his power fails," Calvin remarks.[57] This, for once, really is a zero-sum game.

Though he dismisses as speculative many of its stereotypical questions, Calvin's own systematic doctrine does still rehearse the core traditional claims about the devil as fallen angel willfully corrupted by privative evil, existing and operating under divine providence and permission, and indeed does so under the rubric of "The Knowledge of God the Creator" within Book I of the *Institutes*.[58] Yet, perhaps surprisingly, here as in his *Catechisms*, Calvin allows his doctrinal interest to be drawn beyond the confines of the first article—as important as it may be—firmly into the second article, where Christ and his saving work are the heart of the matter. As Karlfried Fröhlich observes, "the archetypal motif of [Israel's] prophetic faith reappears" notably in Calvin's theology: God in Christ contends with Satan, a salutary contest which takes shape in the world as the reign of God wrests away the devil's power.[59] Arguably it is finally biblical pressure that drives both Calvin and the authors of the *Heidelberg Catechism*—and centuries later Karl Barth as well—to integrate discourse about the devil into some of their most fundamental descriptions of the work and outworking of salvation.[60] In picking up these motifs, this parallel tradition and dogmatic "minority report" wagers that our doctrine can and should do just what Schleiermacher denied

[57] Calvin, *Institutes* (1559) 1.14.18

[58] Calvin, *Institutes* (1559) 1.14.3, 16, 17. As to questions about the timing of the devil's fall, its causes, and its conditions of possibility in the metaphysics of angelic being, Calvin says: "But because this has nothing to do with us, it was better [for scripture] not to say anything" (1.14.16).

[59] Karlfried Fröhlich, *Gottesreich Welt und Kirche bei Calvin: Ein Beitrag zur Frage nach dem Reichgottesglauben Calvins* (Verlag Ernst Reinhardt, 1930), 19.

[60] Calvin's account in the *Institutes* is largely an expansive gloss on prominent Gospel passages about the devil.

was possible: namely, it can and should acknowledge the devil as a figure essentially ingredient in and salient to the understanding of our redemption and the manner of its outworking.

CONCLUSIONS AND ANTICIPATIONS

What would be involved if we were to take up this minority report and join in making this particular wager? What if we were to allow our thinking and speaking of the devil to take its primary impulses and orientation from squarely within the second article of the creed, i.e., with formative reference to the person and work of the Savior? What if (*pace* Schleiermacher) it turns out that the discourse about the devil is not merely incidental to the gospel and the gospel's portrait of Jesus Christ, but integral to it, and importantly so? Might the devil actually prove to be a figure—mythic, poetic, storied, to be sure, but with no less purchase on reality for being so, one of those crucial "ontological metaphors"—which we need to think and to speak evangelically of evil—i.e., to think and to speak of evil in terms of and as determined by the gospel of God and thus concretely within the work of Christian doctrine—and so also, in just this way, to speak the gospel itself?

The remainder of this book will explore precisely this prospect in some detail, pressing questions about the form, content, and significance of diabology along the way. My approach is guided by Karl Barth's maxim that "demonology is in fact only a negative reflection of biblical Christology and soteriology" and Heinrich Vogel's related claim that any properly dogmatic approach to the devil must conceive of him only in his inimical confrontation with and counterpoint to Christ.[61] In keeping with these principles, the three chapters that follow adopt a recurrent form. Each will begin with exegetical reflection upon materials from the Gospels in which the confrontation of Christ and the devil is rendered concretely. We will consider in turn diabolic temptation, diabolic possession, and diabolic falsehood. These aspects of the devil's portrait will be conceived and exposited as assaults upon and contradictions of Christ's threefold

[61] Barth, *Church Dogmatics* III/3, 530. Cf. Heinrich Vogel, *Gott in Christo: Ein Erkenntnisgang durch die Grundprobleme der Dogmatik*, Teil 2, *Heinrich Vogel Gesammelte Werke*, Band 2 (Radius Verlag, 1982), 594. In the tradition of modern European dogmatics, Barth, Vogel, and also Helmut Thielicke might be the outliers in their direct and at times revisionist treatment of the devil in their dogmatics.

identity and saving work as the Way, the Life, and the Truth. In this way I hope to build up a decidedly anti-christological portrait of the devil—a portrait in negative relief, as it were—and to reflect upon the concretion of diabolical evil as in turn insurgent, deadly, and false. This will allow us to consider the specific quality of our redemption from this same threefold evil (i.e., from false lordship, from death, and from lies) and then in turn to reflect upon the Christian life this deliverance secures and the struggle it enjoins. Overall, what will emerge across these next chapters is a cumulative account of the being and agency of the devil as *adventitious*, *adversarial*, and *anarchic* and of the Christian life as parabolic resistance to evil in pursuit of freedom, flourishing, and fidelity. The next chapter begins this cycle by reflecting upon the Messiah's confrontation with diabolical temptation.

3
SATANIC TEMPTATION—MESSIANIC VOCATION

The devil can cite Scripture for his purpose.

The Merchant of Venice, Act I, scene 3

Readers of the previous chapter were led through a highly compressed sketch of certain key aspects of the development of the devil as a theme in Western Christian doctrine. The upshot of that sketch was to suggest that dogmatic interest in the devil has typically been predominated by the concerns of angelology and interest in it largely exhausted within the confines of the first article of the creed, i.e., in relation to matters of creation and providence. We traced a doctrinal tradition of asking and answering what became a rather tight circle of stereotypical questions that ran up and into the modern period with only minor variations. Amongst the Reformed it fell to Schleiermacher to call time on this line of the tradition. He did so on both logical and exegetical grounds, but also in recognition of just how remote and insignificant it had become for theological reflection upon the central Christian concern of salvation.

I suggested, however, that another pattern of dogmatic interest in the question of the devil could also be discerned, a kind of "minority report," which seated theological interest in the theme firmly in the center of soteriology. We espied this in the central material claims of

Barth's doctrine of nothingness and in aspects of John Calvin's teaching, and it was also clearly visible in the theology of the *Heidelberg Catechism*, one of the most enduring instruments of Christian instruction in the Reformed tradition. Encouraged and oriented by this minority report, I proposed revisiting the motif of the devil in this line, exploring what might be made of the theme if we were to approach it afresh with a particular christological and soteriological concentration.

And so here we are. The task of the next three chapters of this study requires somewhat of a shift in task and tone compared to what has gone before. Each of these three central chapters bears a common form. Each opens with an exegetical provocation drawn from the Gospels. Insights won from that work then drive theological reflections on specific aspects of the identity, ontology, and agency of the devil. These are themselves worked out in close contact with particular aspects of the person and work of Christ. Here in chapter 3 the devil is cast as an antagonist of Christ's messianic identity as "the Way." In chapter 4, he appears as the opponent of Christ as "the Life." In chapter 5, the devil emerges as the enemy of Christ as "the Truth." Each of these chapters ends with a closing excursus which comments concisely on implications of all this for understanding the Christian life. The hope is to reacquaint ourselves with the figure of the devil precisely in the soteriological context afforded by the "second article" of the creed. In this context we will meet him as the agent of a manifold repudiation of the specific forms of divine saving grace and will be able to build up the devil's portrait precisely as the worker of *these* inimical works. Painting this portrait will take several sittings, as it were, of which this chapter is but the first of three. I beg the patience of my readers as the composition comes together.

Let us begin then with temptation.

THE GOSPEL: ITS ADVERSARY—EXEGETICAL PROVOCATIONS

Jesus's temptation in the wilderness is attested in all three of the Synoptic Gospels. Standing at the outset of his public ministry, it tells of his first step along the way of his calling and serves as a kind of prelude. And like an operatic prelude, this incident anticipates some of the most important motifs of the longer drama to come. It also represents the devil's first and dramatic appearance in the Gospel accounts.

Mark's Gospel at first blush seems only to have an independent knowledge of—or interest in—the mere "that" of Jesus's temptation as his very brief account suggests: "And the Spirit immediately drove him out into the wilderness. He was in the wilderness forty days, tested by Satan, and he was with the wild beasts, and the angels waited on him" (Mark 1:12–13). Yet, that is not quite right. For the forceful impetus (the Spirit), the hostile location (desert wilderness), the symbolic duration ("forty days"), the witnesses (wild animals), the support (angels), and the adversary (Satan), are all specified. Here too Satan—the "transcendent accuser and adversary of God's people"[1]—gets a first verb: namely, "to test" most commonly but also "to tempt," but also perhaps finally "to seduce," "to try" (as in "trying times"), and so "to press" or "put under pressure." So, the encounter inaugurates a struggle, what Ched Myers famously styled an apocalyptic campaign of the Spirit and the Spirit-led Jesus (on the one side) against Satan, and the demon usurped world (on the other).[2] The desert is an arena in which the "powerful Spirit of God . . . at work in him now immediately confronts the transcendent power of evil."[3] The encounter is purposed to vanquish the devil, to see him driven from the field.[4] The terseness of Mark's report seems to trade away detail in order to stress instead just "the implacable hostility between the two combatants," as one commentator explains.[5]

Though likely building upon the sayings source rather than Mark, the other Synoptic accounts of Jesus's temptation also stage the

1 M. Eugene Boring, *Mark: A Commentary*, New Testament Library (Westminster John Knox, 2006), 47.

2 Ched Myers, *Binding the Strong Man: A Political Reading of Mark's Story of Jesus*, 20th anniversary ed. (Orbis, 2008). The whole reading turns around an account of Mark's telling of Jesus's story as an "apocalyptic combat myth" which runs simultaneously in a sociopolitical register in virtue of the story serving to reproduce social conflict symbolically, i.e., Jesus's actions are always also *symbolic* actions of this kind (pp. 165, 142–43).

3 Boring, *Mark*, 47–48. Cf. Ulrich W. Mauser, *Christ in the Wilderness: The Wilderness Theme in the Second Gospel and Its Basis in the Biblical Tradition* (SCM, 1963).

4 In the parallel text of the Testament of Naphtali, God pledges to appear to save Israel so that "the devil will flee from you / wild animals will be afraid of you / and the angels will stand by you" (T. Naph. 8:3–4).

5 Joel Marcus, *Mark 1–8*, Anchor Bible (Doubleday/Yale University Press, 2000), 167.

encounter as an inaugural confrontation with the adversary.[6] Luke's expansive version runs like this:

> Jesus, full of the Holy Spirit, returned from the Jordan and was led by the Spirit in the wilderness, where for forty days he was tested by the devil. He ate nothing at all during those days, and when they were over, he was famished. The devil said to him, "If you are the Son of God, command this stone to become a loaf of bread." Jesus answered him, "It is written, 'One does not live by bread alone.'" Then the devil led him up and showed him in an instant all the kingdoms of the world. And the devil said to him, "To you I will give their glory and all this authority; for it has been given over to me, and I give it to anyone I please. If you, then, will worship me, it will all be yours." Jesus answered him, "It is written, 'Worship the Lord your God, and serve only him.'" Then the devil took him to Jerusalem and placed him on the pinnacle of the temple, saying to him, "If you are the Son of God, throw yourself down from here, for it is written, 'He will command his angels concerning you, to protect you,' and 'On their hands they will bear you up, so that you will not dash your foot against a stone.'" Jesus answered him, "It is said, 'Do not put the Lord your God to the test.'" When the devil had finished every test, he departed from him until an opportune time. (Luke 4:1–13)[7]

Again, in this telling the Spirit *hurls* its chosen one into a confrontation with the enemy. They meet on the enemy's terrain, the wilderness. The vocabulary suggests the devil does not so much test as *tempt* and *press* with hostile rather than pedagogical intent.[8] The whole scene evokes at once the image of the first human pair beguiled and misled by serpentine questions in the garden, but also of Israel and its prophet leaders in the wilderness, their course threatened to be

[6] John Kloppenborg Verbin, *Excavating Q: The History and Setting of the Sayings Gospel* (T&T Clark, 2000), 100. See discussion in Dale C. Allison Jr., *The Jesus Tradition in Q* (Trinity Press International, 1997), 8–11.

[7] Cf. parallel in Matt 4:1–11, which varies the order of the last two temptations and lacks the closing comment about the devil leaving off "until an opportune time."

[8] Francois Bovon, *Luke 1: A Commentary on the Gospel of Luke 1:1–9:50*, ed. H. Koester, trans. Christine M. Thomas, Hermeneia (Fortress, 2002), 141. Cf. Roy Yates, "Jesus and the Demonic in the Synoptic Gospels," *Irish Theological Quarterly* 44, no. 1 (1977): 40.

derailed by parallel contests about food security, unwise experiments in tactical idolatry, and the desire for evidence on demand of the faithfulness of God.[9]

At stake with Jesus here is both the "Way of the Lord" that he walks and the "Way of the Lord" that he himself is. Jesus is tempted as Savior, *as* Messiah: "*Granted you are the Son of God . . .*" begins the Satan. Not *whether* Jesus is the Son of God, but rather just *how* and *to what end* Jesus is and will enact his identity as the Son of God is the crux of the matter. In this sense, "it was our salvation that [the devil] attacked in the Person of Christ" when he took up this *conflict* with hostility, forcefulness, and bitterness.[10] Calvin suggests that Satan assaults Christ's own faith in the One who sent him, pushing him to "move away from God and follow the dictates of infidelity," to "experiment upon the power of God without necessity," and to "seek the inheritance which God promised his children other than [from] God's own hands."[11] It seems that Jesus's right relation with the One who sent him *and* his proper relation with those to whom he has been sent are simultaneously pressed upon. As one commentator observes, "Jesus will indeed do miracles later, and even multiply bread (Luke 9:12–17). But he will do it for others, not for himself. If bread had priority over his relationship to the Father, he would have succumbed to temptation. His messianic power would then have been destroyed."[12] In the final temptation of Luke's sequence we see how "Jesus wishes nothing for himself and thus will not put God to the test."[13] In sum, the encounter with the adversary in the wilderness is an ordeal out of which the Messiah shows he "has grasped his identity and vocation as Son of God and that he will not swerve from fidelity to God's ways."[14]

[9] Cf. on this parallel with Israel in the wilderness virtually all commentaries everywhere.

[10] John Calvin, *The Harmony of the Gospels: Matthew, Mark & Luke*, ed. D. W. Torrance and T. F. Torrance, trans. A. V. Morrison, Calvin's New Testament Commentaries (Eerdmans, 1994), 1:135.

[11] Calvin, *Harmony of the Gospels*, 1:137, 141, 142.

[12] Bovon, *Luke 1*, 143.

[13] Bovon, *Luke 1*, 145.

[14] John T. Carroll, *Luke: A Commentary*, New Testament Library (Westminster John Knox, 2012), 101.

To repeat: not *whether* but *how* and *to what end* Jesus is and will enact his identity as Son of God is the point at issue.[15] The heart of the diabolical attack is "the counsel, the suggestion, that [Christ] should not be true to the way on which he entered in Jordan, that of a great sinner repenting"[16] but should instead pursue another way, one which does not have God's commission as its sole source, does not have the salvation of others as its sole aim, and does not have the cross at its terminus. Obedience to the charge of the One who sent him is the channel through which the power of the Spirit driving him must flow. That the "debate" with Satan should turn on texts drawn exclusively from Deuteronomy is telling in this respect. The ultimate target of diabolical temptation is Jesus's positive affirmation—by way of his obedience to the Torah—of the vocation of the "Son of God" ascribed to him at his baptism.[17] Or, said differently, "in all three instances there is *one* temptation," namely the temptation to forfeit trust in the divine word of calling and promise, so that what is really at stake is a "final apostasy from God."[18]

It is meaningful that Luke's telling of Christ's victorious *contretemps* in the desert ends with the observation that "the devil left him until an opportune time." Rather than signaling that the ministry that follows is "devil free,"[19] as has sometimes been suggested, this device actually construes what follows as a life and work threatened by the return of the self-same enemy: in other words, "Jesus' powerful spiritual adversary has not spoken his last word."[20] Christ's entire min-

[15] Cf. W. D. Davies and Dale C. Allison, *Matthew 1–7* (T&T Clark, 1988), 367: "How should Jesus exercise his powers as Son of God? The answer given is, In obedience to God."

[16] Thus Karl Barth, *Church Dogmatics* IV/1, 261.

[17] Ulrich Luz, *Matthew 1–7: A Commentary*, trans. Wilhelm C. Linss (T&T Clark, 1990), 185.

[18] So Dietrich Bonhoeffer, "Bible Study on Temptation, June 20–25, 1938," in *Dietrich Bonhoeffer Works*, vol. 15, *Theological Education Underground, 1937–1940* (Fortress, 2012), 394.

[19] So famously Hans Conzelmann, *The Theology of St. Luke* (SCM, 1982), 27–28. The classic argument advanced in Ernest Best, *The Temptation and the Passion: The Markan Soteriology*, 2nd ed. (Cambridge University Press, 1990) suggests that, for Mark, the temptation in the wilderness is already the conclusive defeat of the devil and that the ministry should be understood as a "making real of a victory already accomplished" (p. 15).

[20] Carroll, *Luke*, 104.

istry is thereby placed under the rubric of this "open conflict" as its interpretative frame. We are to expect to meet the work of the devil as the gospel telling unfolds, and so we do, both in Luke/Acts and in Matthew and Mark.[21]

Crucially for our purposes in this chapter, the temptation narrative is focused specifically upon the struggle over the identity and vocation of the messiah and so is not generalizable: in this way it operates as Christian *haggadah* in the service of Christology, not as exemplary moral paraenesis.[22] That is to say, the passages are primarily concerned with the identity of Jesus. They aim to confront us with the Christ whom we follow after in discipleship, rather than figuring Jesus as a generic moral exemplar for our imitation. So, too, then, is the role of the devil similarly circumscribed. Satan is interesting here specifically in relation to the question of the identity and activity of the messiah. It is notable that the devil appears on the scene in the Gospels first and foremost as *Christ's* adversary. As David Jeffrey observes, "it is as though the fundamental antagonist to God and his creation has been exposed in a face-to-face encounter with the new revealed protagonist of salvation history, the Redeemer."[23]

All this is reprised in a highly condensed form in the later report of Peter's confession and rebuke. In Mark's telling of that event we read:

> Jesus went on with his disciples to the villages of Caesarea Philippi; and on the way he asked his disciples, "Who do people say that I am?" And they answered him, "John the Baptist; and others, Elijah; and still others, one of the prophets." He asked them, "But who do you say that I am?" Peter answered him, "You are the Messiah." And he sternly ordered them not to tell anyone about him. Then he began to teach them that the Son of Man must undergo great suffering and be rejected by the elders, the chief priests, and the scribes, and be killed, and after three days rise again. He said all this quite openly. And Peter took him aside and began to rebuke

21 Susan R. Garrett approaches the whole of Luke/Acts with just this focus in *The Demise of the Devil: Magic and the Demonic in Luke's Writing* (Fortress, 1989).

22 So Luz, *Matthew 1–7*, 190. Cf. Davies and Allison, *Matthew 1–7*, 353. Calvin admits as much when he says that the evangelists' aim is "to bring the whole pattern together to produce a kind of mirror or screen image of those features more useful for the understanding of Christ." Calvin, *Harmony of the Gospels*, 1:139. Cf. also David Lyle Jeffrey, *Luke*, Brazos Theological Commentary on the Bible (Brazos, 2012), 68–69.

23 Jeffrey, *Luke*, 66–67.

> him. But turning and looking at his disciples, he rebuked Peter and said, "Get behind me, Satan! For you are setting your mind not on divine things but on human things." (Mark 8:27–33)[24]

Peter's confession and rebuke as "Satan" are, I think, the hinge on which the whole question of diabolical temptation in fact turns.[25] "Satan" here is an epithet that bespeaks the depth and threat of Peter's contradiction of Jesus's self-description of his messianic performance. The violence of Jesus's rebuke reflects what is at stake here: namely, the truth about the "way of the Lord" in the "way of the Messiah," the direction and dynamics of the outworking of salvation as such.[26] The physicality of the language of the rebuke—"Get behind me, Satan!"—reinforces the notion of devilish temptation as obstruction and hindrance.[27] Peter's presumptive outrage blocks the path—gets "in the way"—of the Messiah rather than following "in the way" of discipleship, of "following after."[28] Matthew makes this explicit when Jesus adds to his rebuke the explanation: "for you are a stumbling block to me" (Matt 16:23).[29]

The confrontation with the tempter here once again centers upon the messianic *means* that are integrally ingredient in the messianic purpose and person, i.e., "exactly how his messianic victory over the forces of evil will be accomplished."[30] The Christ must have a mind only for τὰ τοῦ θεοῦ, exercising his saving power in virtue of his exclusive interest in "the things of God." Elizabeth Shively's insight

24 Cf. Matt 16:13–23; Luke 9:18–22, which curiously lack Peter's rebuke.

25 Adela Yarbro Collins suggests the passage is also the "virtual turning point in the narrative as a whole." *Mark: A Commentary*, ed. Harold Attridge, Hermeneia (Fortress, 2007), 398.

26 See Susan R. Garrett, *The Temptations of Jesus in Mark's Gospel* (Eerdmans, 1998), 82: "In sum, in the Caesarea Philippi episode, Mark permits us to glimpse the power of the forces that seek to lead Jesus astray, and the massive effort required to overcome them. The severity of Jesus's rebuke of Peter in Mark 8:33 corresponds to the magnitude of Jesus's temptation here: the rebuke is sharp because the temptation is profound."

27 Marcus, *Mark 1–8*, 607, also associating this incident directly with the final temptation in the desert in Matthew's telling (Ὕπαγε, Matt 4:10); cf. Torsten Löfstedt, *The Devil, Demons, Judas, and "The Jews": Opponents of Christ in the Gospels* (Wipf and Stock, 2021), 237.

28 See Yarbro Collins, *Mark*, 407.

29 Löfstedt, *Devil, Demons, Judas, and "The Jews,"* 236–39.

30 Joel Marcus, *Mark 8–16*, Anchor Bible (Yale University Press, 2009), 614.

that the epithet "Satan" establishes the devil "as the force behind [Peter's] mindset according to τὰ τῶν ἀνθρώπων and is opposed to τὰ τοῦ θεοῦ" finds support in Joel Marcus's forceful observation that here "to be on the side of humans *qua* humans is to be on the side of Satan and at enmity with God."[31] The final victory of the messiah will take the form of "giv[ing] his life a ransom for many" (Mark 10:45). This faithful form of messianic existence has God's commission as its sole source; it has the salvation of others as its sole aim; and it has the cross at its sole terminus. Such are the true "things of God." The only messianic power that can be exercised "for the redemption of many" is *this* power exercised in *this* way, i.e., the way of the passion.[32]

So, Jesus's sharp rhetoric is at one with reality here; there is here no hyperbole.[33] Peter's suggestion is properly satanic—it is of the enemy—precisely because it reprises the diabolical assault in the wilderness on the faithfulness of Christ to the way of the One who sent him. Peter devilishly opposes "the divine plan by rejecting that the messianic Son of Man must suffer"; his is an obstacle to this narrow way.[34] His is an open denial of the messianic way, the intimation of another way, a different path. Peter *qua* Satan is one who would "nullify" the vocation laid upon Jesus by God, like in the parable of the sower where Satan "comes and takes away the word that has been sown" (Mark 4:15).[35] The devil's work indeed.

All this certainly recalls and distills the earlier wilderness temptation. But it also anticipates Christ's final temptation.

The Mount of Olives and the garden of Gethsemane stand at the far end of the messianic way, the final way station to Golgotha

[31] Elizabeth Shively, *Apocalyptic Imagination in the Gospel of Mark: The Literary and Theological Role of Mark 3:22–30* (De Gruyter, 2012), 231–32; Marcus, *Mark 8–16*, 609.

[32] All this could also be drawn from the Fourth Gospel from which the language of Christ as "the Way" is of course drawn, and where Jesus's way to the Father just is the Way of the Cross. Cf. Craig R. Koester, "Jesus as the Way to the Father in Johannine Theology (John 14:6)," in *Theology and Christology in the Fourth Gospel*, ed. G. van Belle et al. (Peeters, 2005), 117–33.

[33] Mauser, *Christ in the Wilderness*, 131–32: "The forthright appellation of Peter as Satan is not a hyperbolic figure of speech. Through the lack of faith on the part of the disciples, Jesus meets the insinuation of evil even in the very midst of his followers."

[34] Yarbro Collins, *Mark*, 407. Cf. B. A. E. Osborne, "Peter: Stumbling-Block and Satan," *Novum Testamentum* 15, no. 3 (1973): 188.

[35] Yarbro Collins makes this connection in *Mark*, 252, 407.

Indeed, we might actually do well to think of the wilderness temptation, Peter's rebuke, and the struggle in Gethsemane as one extended event, one episode of temptation.[36] The devil is unnarrated in this final scene. Yet, the tempter is there in the echo of the satanic voice from the wilderness, the echo of the satanic voice of Peter. The struggle with this interior echo is what calls for anguished prayer, and for the help of the disciples:

> And going a little farther, he threw himself on the ground and prayed that, if it were possible, the hour might pass from him. He said, "Abba, Father, for you all things are possible; remove this cup from me; yet not what I want, but what you want." . . . And again he went away and prayed, saying the same words. (Mark 14:35–36, 39)

This then is the last reprise of the adversary's temptation of the Messiah: Lord, could it not be otherwise than this? Must he be "handed over to sinners"; must the way lead him "to suffer and be rejected by the elders, the chief priests, and the scribes and be killed"? Once more, the possibility of being "messiah by other means" is held out. Understanding well, it seems, that "to will the end is to will the means," diabolical temptation works to forestall the end by disrupting the means, by diverting the way. From Gethsemane to Golgotha, a final diabolical shadow passes over the process of "learning and relearning Jesus' identity" in Mark's Gospel. That shadow is the horrifying threat that Jesus himself might yet be tempted to *unlearn* his own identity as the Christ.[37]

The derisive taunts of the bystanders to the crucifixion to "save himself" and "come down from the cross" (Mark 15:29–32) offer a last embittered invitation to just such *unlearning*, a final satanic temptation to leave off the way, to forestall the eschatological hour with its judgment.[38] To this extent, we might take the climax of Nikos Kazantzakis's controversial novel *The Last Temptation of Christ* as an

[36] Mauser, *Christ in the Wilderness*, 128–32, explores the semantic and conceptual connections between the garden and the wildness.

[37] The phrase is from Beverly Roberts Gaventa, "Learning and Unlearning the Identity of Jesus from Luke-Acts," in *Seeking the Identity of Jesus: A Pilgrimage*, ed. Beverly Roberts Gaventa and Richard B. Hays (Eerdmans, 2008), 164.

[38] Cf. Garrett, *Temptations of Jesus in Mark's Gospel*, 134; Marcus, *Mark 8–16*, 985–89.

insightful exercise in "re-written Scripture," in which the final satanic attack on Jesus's fidelity assumes the form precisely of an alluring dreamlike vision of a different, non-cruciform, un-messianic future.[39]

The devilish temptation of Jesus in the wilderness, in Peter's rebuke, and before the cross are all of a piece because the devil's temptation aims singularly to twist, to question, to qualify, and so to corrode and finally to betray Jesus's own living trust in God's word and promise by proffering another way of being Christ, another vocation, another identity than the Bethlehem to Golgotha existence. Precisely where God calls "Christ, in his humanity and in his divinity, to enact his freedom in a way that results in his crucifixion," the devil suggests things can and should be *otherwise*.[40]

THE SAVIOR: HIS ADVERSARY—DIABOLOGICAL RUMINATIONS

These few exegetical observations have as their purpose to stir us to think of the devil in concrete contact and contradiction of Jesus the Christ, the One who is "*the Way*, and the Truth, and the Life" (John 14:6a).[41] The diabolical work of temptation, we have seen, is directed specifically and consistently as an assault upon Jesus's messianic identity and vocation. The true movement of the Messiah is *from* God, *for* us and our salvation, and *toward* the cross, i.e., a fidelity to God for our sake whose form is self-giving unto death. "For I have come down from heaven," as is said, "not to do my own will, but the will of him who sent me" (John 6:38). The devil's work tempts not to moral malfeasance, or to carnal indulgence, but rather to the "unlearning" and "unwilling of messiah," we might say. It is anti-Christ in the strictest sense. The identity of the Savior is at stake in the question as to whether Jesus can and will make his way in *this* way. The question of the way is as serious as that of the

[39] Nikos Kazantzakis, *The Last Temptation of Christ*, trans. P. A. Bien (Faber and Faber, 1979), 454ff. "Temptation had captured him for a split-second and led him astray. The joys, the marriages and children were lies; the decrepit degraded old men who shouted coward, deserter, traitor at him were lies. All—all were illusions sent by the Devil" (p. 507).

[40] Paul Dafydd Jones, "Karl Barth on Gethsemane," *International Journal of Systematic Theology* 9, no. 2 (2007): 159.

[41] For discussion see Christophe Chalamet, "'Je suis le chemin, la vérité et la vie' (Jn 14,6)," *Revue d'Histoire et de Philosophie Religieuses* 99, no. 1 (2019): 99–111.

destination; indeed, they are indistinguishable. For in this saving work the messianic means are ingredient in and inalienable from the messianic end. As one commentator observes, "Jesus says 'I am the way' (Jn 14:6) after he has spoken about going the way himself (Jn 14:4). Put simply, by going the way of the cross and resurrection Jesus comes to embody the way of the cross and resurrection. To call Jesus 'the way' is to call him 'the Crucified and Risen One.'"[42] There is and can be no messiah by other means. There can be no coming of the kingdom of God in accordance with or conformed to the schemas of the kingdoms of this world.[43]

The devil appears in temptation not as angel but as adversary, *the* adversary of the Christ. The approach we are taking to the devil here involves making our theological reason patient upon just these sorts of concrete oppositional encounters with the Savior. In narrating these encounters, we find that the Gospels are more interested in the devil's *operation* than his origin; they show no interest in where the devil might be from or what the devil might be for but they are fixed instead firmly upon what he is *against*. As the tempter, what he is against is "The Way." The devil *is* enmity, enmity against the way of humble self-giving by which the Christ of God draws near and comes low to save. The devil is that enemy who would have it be *otherwise*.

The devil's attack on the Messiah and the Messiah's way is first and foremost an attack upon the humility and humanity of God, a repudiation of the condescending movement of saving divine grace, of divine mercy, of divine love. And so we stress again how the devil appears as anti-Christ in the plainest sense, i.e., as categorically set against the outworking of Jesus's messianic identity and mission of the Son of God.[44] Unlike the spiritual testing that comes from God, diabolic temptation serves no pedagogical purpose, it "adds no value," it is strictly good for nothing. Rather, it

[42] Koester, "Jesus as the Way to the Father," 128.

[43] John 18:36: "Jesus answered, 'My kingdom does not belong to this world. If my kingdom belonged to this world, my followers would be fighting to keep me from being handed over to the Jews. But as it is, my kingdom is not from here.'"

[44] We could develop this further by imagining how temptation aims to disrupt the Messiah's course by attacking the humanity of its divine movement, and the divinity of its human movement.

aims only at destruction, the deflecting and arresting of the way of the Lord.[45]

The tempter's war against "the Way" also casts a different light upon the nature of the "exclusivity" of that Way. When Jesus says of himself that "no one comes to the Father except by me," we may now hear less an assertion of the gatekeeping function of an apparatus of salvation, and more an insistence upon the *specificity* of the Messiah's identity and agency. God draws near to save wayward and despoiled creatures in *this* way. The exclusivity of the Way is the uniqueness and concreteness of God's own path to us, the specific humility of *this* way, the specific *kenosis* of its form (Phil 2), the particular and gratuitous freedom of its self-giving. The devil's assault on Jesus as "the way" is an assault upon his messianic identity, a refusal that Christ should be truly *this* God, truly *this* human. Perhaps in just this sense the contest also concerns authority, i.e., a calling into question by the devil of the self-authenticating (*autopistis*) character of Christ as divine self-revelation.[46]

We would do well also to note how in the gospel telling the devil's enmity and assault upon the way of the messiah takes place as a reaction, or rear-guard action. The genuine initiative in the narrative lies with God in Christ: it is the Spirit-driven Christ who walks out into the wilderness arena to confront Satan there; it is Christ's own testimony to the Way of the Cross that evokes Peter's satanic rebuke; and it is Jesus's "going up into Jerusalem" in obedience that elicits the last temptations manifest first in self-questioning and then in public derision. This recurrent pattern in which Christ actively confronts the ensconced devil invites us to acknowledge the protagonist of the Gospels as Christ Jesus *agonistes*; they attest that Jesus is the Christ precisely in and by his active contestation of this enemy; this *agon* is ingredient in his messianic identity.[47] He is the One whose gracious ways and works first elicit diabolical resistance and then overreach it.

45 It is not a temptation to more or less (of degree), but a temptation to yes or no, all or nothing (of kind).

46 Cf. Garrett, *Demise of the Devil*, 38–43, where the authority of Christ and that of Satan are made central to the interpretation of the temptation narrative.

47 James G. Kallas, *The Significance of the Synoptic Miracles* (SPCK, 1961), 85: "The life and work of Jesus was a life and death battle with the forces of evil which had seized the world."

All this comports with what commentators sometimes style the "pessimism abroad in late antiquity" which was inclined to take Satan to be "the god of this world" (2 Cor 4:4).[48] As the Johannine Letters have it: "The whole world lies under the power of the evil one" (1 Jn 5:19). Though the next two chapters will bring this out more fully, already here we see the cogency of a certain apocalyptic characterization of incarnation as invasion, of the advent of Christ as a counterinsurgency, of the coming of salvation as a truly divine and truly human movement against "the powers that be" and the entrenched antithetical power behind the powers that be, namely, the illicit "ruler of this world." The devil who tempts Christ seems "with sacrilegious audacity" to have seized "God's earthly dominion to himself as usurper."[49] And so, from beginning to end, Jesus's way is "an uninterrupted confrontation with the devil's might."[50]

In sum, the devil *just is* that inimical power countered by Christ "in" the wilderness, met "in" the person of Peter at Caesarea Philippi, and confronted "in" the mind of Jesus in Gethsemane. In tracing this line of temptation, we have met the devil "in act." This line is reticent concerning the nature of devilish *being*. Yet Peter's rebuke, if not reduced merely to rhetoric, is perhaps suggestive on this score: "Satan" here appears as something that can overlay another—in this case Peter—to the point of (perhaps episodic) paradoxical identity in act. But again, what the name finally picks out is chiefly the sharp antithesis—the contradiction—of the advent and movement and truth of messianic grace. The tempter, we should say, is both *adversarial* and *adventitious* then.

We might venture a further observation here. One thing that is particularly noteworthy, I think, is the role of *language* as a medium of diabolical action. And not just language but even the language of Scripture itself. In these confrontations between Christ and the adversary, not just concepts but actual language—with all of its attendant affect, sociality, history, physicality, passion—is a crucial site of diabolical engagement. The very same language that serves as the medium of divine promise, call, and command is also the field and tool of diabolical temptation. The devil is a hermeneut and a rhetor;

48 The phrase is from Davies and Allison, *Matthew 1–7*, 371.

49 Calvin, *Harmony of the Gospels*, 1:142.

50 Mauser, *Christ in the Wilderness*, 132.

the Edenic serpent his archetype; the temptations of Christ, just so many reiterations of the primal question: "*Did God really say? Did God really mean?*" We can imagine the voice in Gethsemane, whispering: "But teacher, you yourself said, 'For God all things are possible' (Matt 19:26); can the One who sent you not then take away this cup from you, free you from this hour?" We will have more to say about this in chapter 5 when considering the confrontation between divine truth and devilish lies, but what is evident already is that the devil constitutes an *intimate* enemy, one at home in the very sources of faith. Piety as such is not protection from the devil so much as it is the devil's playground.

THE CHRISTIAN LIFE: OUR ADVERSARY—RESISTING THE DEVIL

To round out our reflections on the devil as the enemy of the messianic way of Jesus, let me make two brief observations about the bearing all this might have upon our understanding of the Christian life as a life set under the promise: "Resist the devil, and he will flee" (Jas 4:7). The first concerns the Lord's Prayer.

Prayer is an act of faithfulness and service which—by grace and the Spirit—answers humanly to the faithfulness and service of the Savior. Accounting for Christ's diabolical temptation as we have presses upon what it means for the Christian community to pray with fierce regularity not to be "led into temptation" and to be delivered "from the evil one."[51] It firmly links these two petitions, making them mutually interpreting, perhaps even equating them. It positions us and our struggles within Christ's own struggle for us. The devil is our adversary *because* he is Christ's; he is the enemy of our vocation because he has been the enemy of his. In its gloss on this petition, the *Heidelberg Catechism* explains that, fragile and incessantly assailed as we are by "our deadly enemies, the devil, the world and our own flesh," we can only pray that God mercifully "preserve and strengthen us by the power of [the] Holy Spirit, that we may make firm stand against them and not be overcome in this spiritual warfare, until finally complete victory is ours."[52] The deliverance we seek is the liberty to keep

[51] Note well Christ's prayer (John 17:15): "I am not asking you to take them out of the world, but I ask you to protect them from the evil one."

[52] *Heidelberg Catechism* Q127.

faith with the One who is "the Way," who, though tempted, kept faith with God for our sake. We would be delivered from conspiring against the promise and claim of the humble self-giving of the Christ, to be delivered from "playing Peter," as it were. To pray like this is to disbelieve the devil and so to refuse to worry—or to wish—that Jesus and his messianic way were *otherwise*.

The second observation concerns the Lord's Supper. Our account of Christ's diabolical temptation presses upon what it means for the congregation to celebrate the Supper "remembering Christ" and "proclaiming his death until he comes again." The Supper should be conceived as a locus of Christian resistance to temptation. It is this precisely because in its celebration we—by grace and Spirit—acknowledge the humble self-giving of the Messiah in the concrete form in which he gives himself to us. It reminds us that the way of divine love and mercy is the Way of the Cross—the way of Christ's costly fidelity to the One who sent him for the sake of the blessing of those to whom and for whom he came. The specific identity of the Messiah—the unimpeachable integrity of his unique way and incomparable work—is the special object of our eucharistic remembrance and thanksgiving. To remember this death, then, is to remember its saving purpose and point. It is to be about the business time and time again of "learning and relearning the identity of Jesus" in a world and church tempted to "unlearning." The "sacrifice of praise" made at the table of the Lord's Supper involves our own first steps in walking on the Way, and just so, our own resistance to the devil's temptation for us to walk forgetfully and *otherwise*.

To the quite specific form of Christ's victory over diabolical temptation, then, there corresponds a militant church which prays to be delivered from the temptation of the evil one, a church which remembers in bread and wine the messianic Way of the Cross. To seek *this* gift and undertake *this* action is to resist the devil as disciples of the Way.

CONCLUSIONS AND ANTICIPATIONS

The theological experiment we are undertaking in diabology construes it as a "negative reflection of biblical Christology and soteriology" and so something best pursued by reflecting upon the specific shape and dynamism of the devil's "inimical confrontation with and counterpoint to Christ." This chapter's consideration of the depiction of diabolical temptation threaded through the Gospels has been a modest first effort in this direction. Expositing temptation as a focused, inimical assault upon Jesus's messianic identity as "the Way" has begun to fill out our negative "shadow portrait" or "image in relief" of the devil and his works, highlighting at the same time the fundamentally *agonistic* quality of the Savior's vocation. From it, we also won some initial insights into the Christian life as life marked by prayer for deliverance from diabolical temptation and celebration of the ordinance of the Lord's Supper in grateful remembrance of the way of *this* Christ to the cross for us.

I hope that already these few reflections upon the salience of diabolical temptation have gone some way in substantiating claims like those made by T. W. Manson, that the "demonological element in the gospel is not a mere veneer. It is not a temporary trapping which can be stripped away from the gospel. It is engrained in its very substance. It is needed to bring out its sense."[53] The argument to come will present further opportunities to see how this claim might be borne out, and how its significance for our theology might be acknowledged and owned. To that end, our next chapter will focus in particular upon how the portrait of the devil is filled out further when we attend to the place of demonic possession, exorcism, and deliverance in the Gospel portraits of the Savior Jesus Christ as "the Life."

[53] T. W. Manson, "Principalities and Powers: The Spiritual Background of the Work of Jesus in the Synoptic Gospels," *SNTS Bulletin* 3 (1952): 15.

4
DIABOLICAL POSSESSION—KINGDOM DELIVERANCE

Christ invades the realm of Satan and lays hold of those who belong to him.[1]

Dietrich Bonhoeffer

I will contend with those who contend with you.

Isaiah 49:24–25

In keeping with our approach to diabology as something best pursued by reflecting upon the specific shape and dynamism of the devil's "inimical confrontation with and counterpoint to Christ," the previous chapter began to build up our "portrait in relief" of the figure of the devil. It did so by reflecting specifically upon the diabolical *temptation* of Christ. This temptation we saw to be an inimical assault upon Jesus's messianic vocation, identity, and work as these are summed up in his self-characterization as "the Way." The operation of the devil, we argued, aimed to disrupt or arrest the outworking of salvation by diverting Christ's way to the cross. We won some insight into both the essentially *adversarial* quality of the devil and the *agonistic* character of the Savior's vocation. We ended by considering

[1] Dietrich Bonhoeffer, *Discipleship*, vol. 4 of *Dietrich Bonhoeffer Works*, ed. Geffrey B. Kelley and John D. Godsey, trans. Barbara Green and Reinhard Krauss (Fortress, 2003), 207.

how thinking of diabolical temptation in this way affords a distinct perspective on the Christian life, informing our understanding of daily prayer for deliverance from evil and celebration of the Lord's Supper as forms of resistance to diabolical temptation so understood.

In this present chapter we continue to paint our dogmatic portrait of the devil. The American novelist Flannery O'Connor famously characterized the subject of her fiction as "the action of grace in territory held largely by the devil."[2] In telling the story of Jesus as they do, the evangelists similarly also make "the action of grace in territory held largely by the devil" their fundamental subject matter. We confront this directly as we move from the motif of temptation now to consider the theme of *possession* and to concentrate our attention upon the theological significance of the Gospels' depiction of Jesus Christ as exorcist. Once again, we begin with some exegetical considerations, before moving on that basis to reflect—always in close contact with christological and soteriological considerations—upon the identity, ontology, and agency of the adversary. For reasons which will become clear, in this lecture we connect our diabological thinking in particular to Christ's identity as "The Life." Some brief reflections about the Christian life—in particular about the significance of these themes of possession and exorcism for understanding the practice of baptism and our daily prayer for the coming of the kingdom of God—will round out the chapter.

THE GOSPEL: ITS ADVERSARY—EXEGETICAL PROVOCATIONS

As Dale Allison observes, the historical record tells plainly that Jesus and his disciples engaged in exorcistic activity; more than that, the evidence of the New Testament witness suggests "not only that Jesus was an exorcist but also that he and others saw his ministry in its entirety as a victorious combat with Satan."[3] Although the term

2 Flannery O'Connor, "On Her Own Work," in *Mystery and Manners: Occasional Prose* (Farrar, Straus & Giroux, 1969), 118.

3 Dale C. Allison Jr., "The Historians' Jesus and the Church," in *Seeking the Identity of Jesus: A Pilgrimage*, ed. Beverly Roberts Gaventa and Richard B. Hays (Eerdmans, 2008), 85. For wide-ranging discussion of the theme see Loren Stuckenbruck, "Satan and Demons," in *Jesus Among Friends and Enemies: A Historical and Literary Introduction to Jesus in the Gospels*, ed. Chris Keith and Larry W. Hurtado (Baker Academic, 2011), 173–97.

"exorcist" as such is almost nonexistent in the New Testament,[4] the phenomenon it designates is both widely attested and (for "we moderns") awkwardly prominent in Jesus's life and work, forming an integral part of all three Synoptic portraits. Such exorcistic practice itself is encompassed by what one scholar calls the "recrudescence of Jewish demonology" that took place during the Second Temple period.[5] The biblical and historical scholarship treating this theme in context is correspondingly vast.[6]

The several reported exorcisms of Jesus reported in the Gospels bear much in common. First, they open with the presentation of someone "possessed" or "burdened" or "suffering from" an "evil spirit" or "demon" and accompanied by illness, physical impairment, or bodily suffering; rarely—as in the case of the Gerasene demoniac (Luke 8:26–39)—"a person's whole organism and personality seems to be under the control of an invading spirit."[7] Second, note is often made of the associated social ostracism of those afflicted. With or without dialogue, Jesus speaks and the demon is "rebuked," "cast out," or "driven out"; sometimes this speech is imperatival ("Be silent and come out of him!"; Mark 1:25), sometimes merely indicative ("Woman, great is your faith! Let it be done for you as you wish"; Matt 15:28). Third, the departure of the evil spirit is marked by healing and the restitution of wellness.

The practice of exorcism was, it seems, not at all uncommon in that time and place and so Jesus's activity in this regard is not at all

4 Acts 19:13 has the *only* use: ἐξορκιστής.

5 Ida Fröhlich, "Demons and Illness in Second Temple Judaism: Theory and Practice," in *Demons and Illness from Antiquity to the Early-Modern Period*, ed. Siam Bhayro and Catherine Rider (Brill, 2017), 83.

6 For historical discussion see Graham H. Twelftree, *Jesus the Exorcist: A Contribution to the Study of the Historical Jesus* (Mohr Siebeck, 1993); Otto Böcher, *Christus Exorcista: Dämonismus und Taufe im Neuen Testament* (Kohlhammer, 1972); Andreas Hauw, *The Function of Exorcism Stories in Mark's Gospel* (Wipf and Stock, 2019), esp. the introduction, 1–22, and ch. 3, "Exorcism in the Jewish Second Temple Literature," 33–58. Cf. Cecilia Wassén and Tobias Hägerland, *Jesus the Apocalyptic Prophet* (T&T Clark, 2021), 129–46. See also Richard H. Bell, *Deliver Us from Evil: Interpretating the Redemption from the Power of Satan in New Testament Theology*, WUNT 216 (Mohr Siebeck, 2007), esp. ch. 2, "Deliverance from Satan in the Exorcisms of Jesus," 66–114.

7 This description of "possession" is drawn from Henry Ansgar Kelly, *The Devil, Demonology, and Witchcraft: The Development of Christian Beliefs in Evil Spirits*, rev. ed. (Doubleday, 1974), 69.

unique. What is distinctive in the evangelical depiction of Jesus as exorcist, however, is that he drives out evil spirits without recourse to the exorcist's standard tool kit: including hymnic and prayer formularies, ritualized incantations, incantation bowls, amulets, figurines, etc.[8] Time and again it is Christ's own authoritative word in the encounter which provides the sole means. Interestingly, the Gospels also take an exclusive interest in and associate Jesus with what we might call active "therapeutic exorcism," i.e., the driving out of demons; notably the evangelists show no interest in "prophylactics" intended to ward off the demonic.[9]

For our purposes, I will concentrate here on the so-called "Beelzebul Controversy" together with the parable of the "Binding of the Strong Man" which accompanies it. This pericope is found with variations in all three Synoptic Gospels and most likely reflects at least some of the aboriginal words of Jesus.[10] Crucially, the parable of the strong man and adjacent sayings are presented as Jesus's self-interpretation of the meaning of his work as exorcist. It is thus uniquely valuable as regards the Evangelists' view of the meaning and import of this work, confronting us with their testimony to "the ineradicable division and fierce enmity between [Jesus] and the demonic forces that hold the human race in thrall and blind it to its true good."[11]

In Mark's Gospel, this exorcism and its interpretative parable come early, in chapter 3, and are intercalated with both the conflicts involving Jesus's family and the "scribes from Jerusalem." The other two gospels place the event later and identify Jesus's detractors as either the Pharisees (Matthew) or just "some of the crowd" (Luke). These

[8] For discussion see Gideon Bohak, "Jewish Exorcism Before and After the Destruction of the Second Temple," in *Was 70 CE a Watershed in Jewish History? On Jews and Judaism Before and After the Destruction of the Second Temple*, ed. Daniel R. Schwartz and Zeev Weiss (Brill, 2011), 277–300. Cf. more broadly Gideon Bohak, *Ancient Jewish Magic: A History* (Cambridge University Press, 2008), 70–142, for discussion of the wider Second Temple period, in which exorcism is prominent. Cf. also Bell, *Deliver Us from Evil*, 72–77.

[9] See Gideon Bohak, "Conceptualizing Demons in Late Antique Judaism," in *Demons and Illness from Antiquity to the Early-Modern Period*, ed. Siam Bhayro and Catherine Rider (Brill, 2017), 123.

[10] John Kloppenborg Verbin, *Excavating Q: The History and Setting of the Sayings Gospel* (T&T Clark, 2000), 100; see also W. D. Davies and Dale C. Allison, *Matthew 8–18* (T&T Clark, 1991), 342.

[11] Joel Marcus, *Mark 1–8*, Anchor Bible (Doubleday/Yale University Press, 2000), 279.

differences are significant in their own ways; but for our purposes what matters is the appearance of Satan at the heart of the debate about the source and significance of Jesus's exorcisms. In Luke's version, the text runs like this:

> Now he was casting out a demon that was mute; when the demon had gone out, the one who had been mute spoke, and the crowds were amazed. But some of them said, "He casts out demons by Beelzebul, the ruler of the demons." Others, to test him, kept demanding from him a sign from heaven. But he knew what they were thinking and said to them, "Every kingdom divided against itself becomes a desert, and house falls on house. If Satan also is divided against himself, how will his kingdom stand?—for you say that I cast out the demons by Beelzebul. Now if I cast out the demons by Beelzebul, by whom do your exorcists cast them out? Therefore they will be your judges. But if it is by the finger of God that I cast out the demons, then the kingdom of God has come to you. When a strong man, fully armed, guards his castle, his property is safe. But when one stronger than he attacks him and overpowers him, he takes away his armor in which he trusted and divides his plunder." (Luke 11:14–22; cf. Matt 12:22–29; Mark 3:23–27)

If we "only have eyes for the devil" as we regard this passage, what do we see? The exorcism itself is tersely reported: possessed, a man has been rendered speechless; without any comment on the means, the demon is "driven out" by Jesus and the man finds his voice. Controversy ensues, though not about the exorcism itself but about the power at work in it. Accusers suggest Jesus may himself be possessed—a suggestion mooted on several other occasions[12]—and so claim that he acts in virtue of a greater demonic power, namely Beelzebul, a Jewish traditional name for "the ruler of demons." In intertestamental background sources, this great evil is and can only be thwarted by "Almighty God" and "the one who descends from the heights" (T. Sol. 6:8).[13] So, too, here: Jesus identifies his work as

[12] Cf. Ulrich Luz, *Matthew 8–20: A Commentary*, trans. James E. Crouch, Hermeneia (Fortress, 2001), 203.

[13] T. Sol. 3:1–6: "I am Beelzeboul, the ruler of demons" (v. 6); cf. 6:1–8: "Then I said, 'Tell me which angel thwarts you.' 'The Almighty God,' he replied. 'He is called by the Hebrews *Patike*, the one who descends from the height; he is (called) by the Greeks *Emmanouel*. I am always afraid of him, and trembling. If anyone adjures me with the oath (called) Elo-I, a great name for his power, I disappear.'"

exorcist with nothing less than the coming of the kingdom of God, the work of the hand or "finger" of God (language that recalls the exodus, cf. Exod 8:19; Matthew has "Spirit of God").[14] In short, *God* is identified as the ultimate protagonist here, acting in the actions of Jesus, "powerfully opposing forces that oppress God's people" and so "liberating them."[15] The conflict finally resolves into one between God and the devil, a contest between two kingdoms, two reigns.[16] Jesus's reply treats Beelzebul and Satan as two proper names for the same antagonist: the ultimate actor behind the manifold malfeasance of all demons and evil spirits; all their malevolent and harmful actions are liable to a single diabolical reduction, as it were.

Notably, the grammar of "Satan" here suggests something oddly multiple, collective, a name comprehending something potentially divisible, a "kingdom," perhaps something, one might say, "legion." Disclosing the internal diversity and complexity of the adversary's operation is, however, not the main thing made manifest in Jesus's exorcisms. Rather, the fact that the "demons" subject to exorcism are marked as allies/expressions of Satan renders each and every exorcism as an action against the devil *as such*. The upshot is "to situate the exorcisms in the context of the combat with Satan and so to make explicit," as Forsyth observes, "that they are variants or transformations of the combat myth."[17] Jesus's messianic exorcisms are not finally isolated events or so many discrete contests of spiritual authority; they are rather what happens when the reign of the Lord is made actual: they are serial skirmishes in a single extended campaign, multiple expressions of a single messianic movement, namely, that of

[14] Cf. Susan R. Garrett, *The Demise of the Devil: Magic and the Demonic in Luke's Writing* (Fortress, 1989), 45: "Whether Luke found the expression in his source or inserted it himself, he surely did not fail to grasp the significance of the allusion."

[15] John T. Carroll, *Luke: A Commentary*, New Testament Library (Westminster John Knox, 2012), 256.

[16] An absolute antithesis is intimated in the Jesus saying, "Whoever is not with me is against me" (Luke 11:23). See David Lyle Jeffrey, *Luke*, Brazos Theological Commentary on the Bible (Brazos, 2012), 258–59, who recalls Luther's view that the human will is ever "occupied" by one master or another, "captive, as slave, a servant, to the will of God, or to the will of Satan," citing *Bondage of the Will* §§25–26.

[17] Neil Forsyth, *The Old Enemy: Satan & the Combat Myth* (Princeton University Press, 1987), 295–96 (wider discussion across pp. 293–97).

the advent of the reign of God at the cost of that of the devil.[18] Their essence is the reality of divine *rescue* and *liberation* from diabolical oppression (cf. Acts 10:38).[19] This is the exclusive focus of evangelical interest in them.

All this is reiterated forcefully and memorably in the "parable of the strong man" with its image of the powerful householder being despoiled after being "assailed" and "overcome" and "bound" by the "one stronger than he."[20] There is little interpretative debate about its sense: as Davies and Allison sum it up: "The house of the strong man is Satan's kingdom. His goods or possessions are the people he has under his sway: those possessed by demons. Jesus frees them through his ministry of exorcism."[21] The whole trope casts the matter in terms taken over from texts in Isaiah: "Can the prey be taken from the mighty, or the captives of a tyrant be rescued? But thus says the LORD: Even the captives of the mighty shall be taken, and the prey of the tyrant be rescued; for I will contend with those who contend with you, and I will save your children" (Isa 49:24–25).[22] This picture holds true for each exorcism as well as for the whole redemptive ministry of Christ of which they are a part. The image of "binding the devil" lends the whole business a decidedly eschatological cast.[23] We can and should take the parable of the strong man as another parable of the kingdom, to be sure. But in its immediate setting it also serves specifically as an "implicit allegory" for Jesus's exorcistic work,

[18] Anton Fridrichsen, "The Conflict of Jesus with Unclean Spirits," *Churchman* 22, no. 129 (1931): 127; repr. in *Exegetical Writings: A Selection*, ed. and trans. Chrys C. Caragounis and Tord Fornberg (Mohr Siebeck, 1994), 71–83. Cf. Elizabeth Shively, *Apocalyptic Imagination in the Gospel of Mark: The Literary and Theological Role of Mark 3:22–30* (De Gruyter, 2012), 49, and Ched Myers, *Binding the Strong Man: A Political Reading of Mark's Story of Jesus*, 20th anniversary ed. (Orbis, 1988).

[19] Shively, *Apocalyptic Imagination in the Gospel of Mark*, 49.

[20] The Matthew and Mark parallels have "bind" as the operative verb here (Mark 3:27; Matt 12:29).

[21] Davies and Allison, *Matthew 8–18*, 342.

[22] Shively, *Apocalyptic Imagination in the Gospel of Mark*, 47; Marcus, *Mark 1–8*, 283; Myers, *Binding the Strong Man*, 167. Cf. Isa 40:10: "See, the Lord GOD comes with might, and his arm rules for him; his reward is with him, and his recompense before him."

[23] See Luz, *Matthew 8–20*, 205 which points up 1 En. 10:4–5; Jub. 48:15, 18; T. Levi 18:12, and canonically in the New Testament Rev 20:2–3.

an explanation of "what is going on" in "what is taking place."[24] What is taking place are Christ's exorcisms; what is going on is the realization of eschatological messianic deliverance, for "something stronger than Satan has bound him," namely, Jesus the "stronger one" of whom John the Baptist spoke (Mark 1:7).[25] This essential link between eschatology and exorcism is what finally makes these events evangelically intelligible. As part of the extended prologue to Christ's passion, as it were, they also tether evangelical discourse of "power" firmly to the Way of the Cross.

Allow me one further brief exegetical observation at this juncture. I noted earlier in passing that the possessed are regularly socially excluded, hidden away, lurking in cemeteries, or in the wilderness, or outside the gates, their suffering thus amplified by social exclusion. Jesus's exorcisms—like his healings more generally—also repeatedly make for social reintegration. The casting out of demons brings with it the casting out of the victim's casting out from the community, as it were. Take but one example: Luke 13:10–17 tells of the healing of a woman afflicted by a demonic "spirit of weakness" and doubled over for eighteen years. Jesus's words and his touch effect a Sabbath day cure, provoking criticism to which Jesus retorts: "And ought not this woman, a daughter of Abraham whom Satan bound for eighteen long years, be set free from this bondage on the Sabbath day?" (Luke 13:16). As one commentator observes, "Where Jesus, the Lord—and Lord of the Sabbath—is present, the present is the time for liberative action. The mandate for action today comes from the reality of God's reign present and powerfully active, countering the harmful domination of Satan, in this moment."[26] So in this instance, one whom Satan had bound is loosed when Satan himself is bound by the "stronger one"; someone initially simply referred to as "a woman" is now acknowledged explicitly as "a daughter of Abraham," a form of address emphasizing her belonging. In this exorcism, Israel's Sabbath in remembrance of liberation becomes an actual Sabbath *for her* as one now restored, set upright. She now

[24] So Marcus, *Mark 1–8*, 282. As regards Luke, so also Garrett, *Demise of the Devil*, 45.

[25] Adela Yarbro Collins, *Mark: A Commentary*, ed. Harold Attridge, Hermeneia (Fortress, 2007), 233–34. Cf. Bell, *Deliver Us from Evil*, 89.

[26] Carroll, *Luke*, 284.

stands among them as a living "parable in person" of the fortunes of the whole of the people of God.[27]

Finally—and crucially—we note that across gospel testimonies to Jesus's exorcisms those possessed are themselves never construed as the enemies of the Lord; they are rather the children of God, sons and daughters of Israel. The enemy of the exorcist is someone, something, other: namely, that uncanny power that has usurped their lives. Jesus and the possessed have a *common* adversary: the true diabolical enemy is a triangulated, third thing. The possessed are not threatening to Jesus, they themselves are not obstacles of the kingdom. They are rather simply those who are particularly oppressed by the demonic; they stand as signs and markers of the difficult fact that human life is yet being lived out in "time organized by death."[28] They suffer acutely under its pressure and disturbance what we all endure. Possession might be thought of as an extreme—and as such also exemplary or paradigmatic—instance of the human condition in the order of sin, a terrible, practical parable of the reign of its diabolical power in and over human life, the usurpation of the good creature and the good creation by forces inimical to them.[29] The exorcistic resolution of the suffering of the possessed is a messianic movement against human misery of the deepest and worst sort. Ending demonic occupation, exorcism brings with it an end to the inhuman misery such possession involves, delivering its subject back into new—and newly human—life.

THE SAVIOR: HIS ADVERSARY—DIABOLOGICAL RUMINATIONS

These few exegetical observations continue to help us to think of the devil in concrete contact and contradiction of Jesus the Christ,

[27] Cf. Michael Wolter, *Das Lukasevangelium* (Mohr Siebeck, 2008), 484–85; cited in Carroll, *Luke*, 286.

[28] See Ann Jervis, *Paul and Time* (Baker Academic, 2023) for discussion of the realm of "death time" as creaturely time "organized by death." Cf. James Kallas, *The Significance of the Synoptic Miracles* (SPCK, 1961), 63: "For Jesus they [demoniacs] were not especially wicked people but supremely unfortunate people. For Jesus, demon possession does not mean a league with Satan but a bondage to Satan."

[29] Cf. Stuckenbruck, "Satan and Demons," 193, who suggests of the Enochic view that the notion of possession may serve in this way as a testimony that "preserves" the dignity of human life in the created order.

the One who is "the Way, the Truth," and—for present purposes in particular—"*the Life*" (John 14:6a).[30] They point up the dramatic content that fills out the axiom of the Fourth Gospel: "The thief comes only to steal and kill and destroy. I came that they may have life, and have it abundantly" (John 10:10). The diabolical work of possession, we have seen, is directed specifically against the welfare and flourishing of the life of God's children, afflicting their bodies, burdening their souls, breaking their community. Here we encounter the devil as a purveyor of misery, one whose *modus operandi* involves oppressing human lives with a terrible and unwelcome *prolepsis* of death. The physical, mental and social harm associated with possession are so many eerie anticipations of death, the reach of its long, cold hand back into the present, as it were. What the devil occupies becomes diminished, depleted, and ultimately dissolved. Such is the virulently dynamic quality of nothingness, of death. The fragility and vulnerability and need integral to human creatureliness are therein exploited and weaponized.[31]

But to what end? Why are the possessed *possessed*? The suffering brought about by such occupation is, it seems, purposeless, set in the service of no definable positive point—it aims at no particular end save perhaps the nihilistic end of disrupting and depleting the lives of the children of God. The contradiction, disruption, and diminishment of creaturely life are here their own "end," as it were. The adversary is, as John's Gospel has it, "a murderer from the beginning" (John 8:44). In this context, we might take that to mean that the relentless dissolution of life involved in demonic possession is its indelible and determining *animus*. If the deadly demonic operation surfaced in the testimony of the Gospels constitutes a "kingdom," then it is a consumptive, pointless, and so anarchic one: it is exhaustively a kingdom of death.

Again, this comes to light precisely in the confrontation with Messiah as the One who is "The Life," the One who comes so that all those oppressed by the devil may have life and have it in abundance. The antithetical willing and working of the devil concretely

[30] For discussion see Christophe Chalamet, "'Je suis le chemin, la vérité et la vie' (Jn 14,6)," *Revue d'Histoire et de Philosophie Religieuses* 99, no. 1 (2019): 99–111.

[31] Do our texts associate possession here with what the tradition calls "natural evils"? How interesting and important might that be for thinking about the quality of natural evil?

contradicts the integrity and vitality of created, covenanted, and rescued human life, and it saps the freedom, responsibility, and worship to which it is called. It does so with both acknowledged reach and breadth as well as alarming intensity and depth. Human bodies, psyches, and community—and so also human politics—all prove to be the field of demonic depletion: the structures of selfhood and of sociality are put at issue, made the targets of devilish undoing. We are reminded here that the devil figures as the antithesis of God *and* of God's good creation and its flourishing. The devil stands in sheer enmity to all this, the antithesis of divine generosity, of the gracious overflow of love from which creation derives, and the opponent of the mercifully appointed ends toward which it is destined. The devil is the enemy of creation and new creation alike.

Importantly, I think, these reflections also forcefully remind us that not only human malfeasance but also human *misery* are the object of Christ's saving work. If we attend to the significance of diabolical possession and messianic exorcism, then our doctrine of salvation will need to be capacious enough to comprehend both repentance *and* rescue, forgiveness and deliverance.

Developing this thought, we could understand Christ's exorcistic work to be primarily addressed to the problem of what Brian Gerrish in his doctrine of sin calls *estrangement*.[32] Gerrish argues that alongside the pride which features prominently in received theologies of sin, we need also to speak and think of sin as estrangement and alienation from both self and others. Our fallen condition, our captivity to sin, comes to expression in willful defiance, yes, but also in "guiltless mistrust" born of betrayal and fear. We lack "blessedness" because we undo ourselves, but also because we have been and are undone; our sinful condition has both active and passive aspects, which are both and together corrosive of human personhood and human community. So, the saving work of Christ is pitched to redeem us from a world whose life is drained and distorted by "willful rebellion . . . [and] self-assertion" but also by mistrust born of what Gerrish calls "depletion of the self."[33] This kind of analysis catches up with important deliverances from feminist reflection on

[32] Brian Gerrish, *The Christian Faith: Dogmatics in Outline* (Westminster John Knox, 2015), 77ff. for chs. 7, "Estrangement," and 8, "God and Evil."

[33] Gerrish, *Christian Faith*, 89.

the problem of sin, and the neglect in our doctrine of attention to the problems of "soluble" selfhood and the sometimes dehumanizing demands for "self-abnegation."[34]

Gerrish's account of sin as estrangement has its own motivations, but our tarrying with the Gospel witness to Jesus Christ as exorcist, I suggest, affords particular reasons to commit to something like it. For we recognize Jesus's practice of exorcism as the merciful movement of God against that afflicting power which would dissolve creaturely life. The problem of possession, we might say, just is the problem of the depleted self, the displaced and dissolute self, the self overrun and effaced by heteronomous powers, and all the misery, distrust, and estrangement that condition enjoins and inflicts. The devil then names the annihilating power at work and at war with the world, inimical to its continuation, its integrity, and its flourishing. That this power is thought to be preternatural comports with our acknowledgment that the problem it presents to us is beyond our ken, and that the work of Jesus Christ as Savior is positively addressed to *this* problem too. If we downplay the prominence of possession and exorcism in the Gospels' portrait of Jesus's ministry, we may also overlook the important place of the recovery and restoration of selfhood and community within the full orb of his saving work, i.e., the way in which the Savior confronts the devilish adversary concretely as "the Life."

From such reflections we might also be provoked to think again about our accounts of the human self. The evangelical narratives of possession with which we have been thinking put immense pressure on our modern commonsense notions of autonomous selfhood, coherent identity, and integral personhood. The "buffered self" of this secular age of ours of which Charles Taylor writes seems impervious by design to the sorts of scenarios in view here.[35] Yet perhaps, as Susan Eastman's important work on cosmology and anthropology in Paul has shown, there are ways (both ancient and modern) of conceiving the self in which identity and personhood are much more malleable, porous, externally interconnected—indeed, inter-subjective—and

[34] For discussion see Lisa E. Dahill, *Reading from the Underside of Selfhood: Bonhoeffer and Spiritual Formation* (Wipf and Stock, 2009), esp. chs. 1 and 4. Cf. Hyun Joo Kim, *Bearing Sin as Church Community: Bonhoeffer's Hamartiology* (T&T Clark, 2022), ch. 6.

[35] See Charles Taylor, *A Secular Age* (Harvard University Press, 2007).

so open and vulnerable to powerful determining connections and communications.[36] Eastman's research suggests it might not be fanciful at all to acknowledge that our selfhood is far less "buffered" and far more permeable to what lies beyond it than we might have previously imagined. Perhaps then the language of "possession" picks out something discernible in our world, not only (or even chiefly) in the extraordinary but also in the ordinary. One could well unfold a searching account of the self as a site of overlapping and contesting powers and possessions, a locus where cultural, linguistic, social, physical, psychic, spiritual, ideological, chemical, virtual, and other powers play themselves out. On such an account, might theology not reach for concepts like "possession" and even "exorcism" precisely in order to come properly to terms with the realities of beset human identity and personhood? Might this prove to be part of that repertoire of "metaphysical poetry" the evangelical traditions put at our disposal?

However that may be, the central role played by possession and exorcism in the outworking of Christ's ministry draws our attention once more to just how agonistic and adversarial is the scriptural telling of the gospel of God. "The world, since the apostasy," wrote Charles Hodge, "belongs to the kingdom of Satan; and to redeem it from his dominion was the special object of the mission of the Son of God."[37] Jesus is evangelically depicted as "an exorcist *par excellence*" and his "counterdemonic manoeuvres fit logically within the framework of an apocalyptic worldview."[38] Jesus's practice of exorcism—understood as we have suggested as sustained campaign in which the *prolepsis* of new, eschatological life overtakes even now those beset by the pressing power of death—also brings us face to face with the unsettled history or "career" of God's good creation. The gospel writers can only conceive of their world as what J. Louis Martyn called a "twice invaded world," i.e., a cosmos invaded once by the inimical and uncanny "anti-God powers" and then again in Christ, by God

[36] See Susan Eastman, *Paul and the Person: Reframing Paul's Anthropology* (Eerdmans, 2017), esp. ch. 3, "Embodied and Embedded," 89ff. See also her *Oneself in Another: Participation and Personhood in Pauline Theology* (Wipf and Stock, 2023).

[37] Charles Hodge, *Systematic Theology*, 3 vols. (1872–73; repr., Eerdmans, 1981), 1:646.

[38] Stuckenbruck, "Satan and Demons," 194.

come low to save.[39] In this way, Jesus's exorcisms are presented as "part of a decisive, coordinated attack on the entire structure of evil in the universe," a further expression of that divine counterinsurgency we noted in the previous chapter.[40] And so the world is acknowledged by faith to be a "theatre of world-palingenesis," which is to say, a site of metamorphosis in which something new is being wrested out of the old, in which eschatological life is erupting in the midst of sovereign death.[41] Individually and taken together, the evangelical exorcisms are parables of just this: they are telling episodes in the overpowering and despoiling of the dissolute usurper and his kingdom of death by the gracious Lord of life—even the One "through whom are all things" (1 Cor 8:6; John 1:3)—for the sake of the new. In word and gesture, Christ exercises "a *dunamis* [a creative power] to which Satan's kingdom"—the world as it is "threatened, plagued and possessed by devils"—"must yield."[42]

In these gospel testimonies we meet Christ as God's own movement against our misery, and against its deepest and most powerful origins and most intractable operations. This divine movement of life against the illicit reign of death finds its term, strangely, in the work of the cross. Eberhard Jüngel spoke insightfully of the event of the cross as "the union of death and life" in God's own life "for the sake of life."[43] We can take this as a gloss on that programmatic

39 See J. Louis Martyn, "World Without End or Twice-Invaded World?" in *Shaking Heaven and Earth: Essays in Honor of Walter Brueggemann and Charles B. Cousar*, ed. Christine Roy Yoder et al. (Westminster John Knox, 2005), 117–32. Cf. J. Louis Martyn, "The Apocalyptic Gospel in Galatians," *Interpretation* 54, no. 3 (2000): 246–66, who rightly draws out how the apostle can, on such grounds, only conceive of the gospel not as "about human movement into blessedness (religion)" but "about God's liberating invasion of the cosmos (theology)."

40 Marcus, *Mark 1–8*, 283. Myers's bifocal reading of Mark's Gospel along these lines via "symbolic representation" of the political receives support perhaps from this claim—the whole "empire of evil" is in view.

41 The phrase "theatre of world-palingenesis" is from Amos Wilder, *Jesus' Parables and the War of Myths* (Fortress, 1982), 34; cited in Myers, *Binding the Strong Man*, 102.

42 Jacob Taubes, *Occidental Eschatology*, trans. David Ratmoko (Stanford University Press, 2009), 50–51. In this Taubes follows Rudolph Otto, *The Kingdom of God and the Son of Man: A Study in the History of Religion*, trans. F. V. Wilson and B. L. Woolf (Lutterworth, 1938), esp. 97–107.

43 Eberhard Jüngel, *God as the Mystery of the World*, trans. D. Guder (T&T Clark, 1983), 299.

passage in Hebrews which declares that "Since the children share flesh and blood, [Christ] himself likewise shared the same things, so that through death he might destroy the one who has the power of death, that is, the devil" (Heb 2:14). These ideas come together in an understanding of the cross as "the great exorcism," the culminating act of redemption, the re-possession of the possessed, the eschatological judgment by which "the ruler of this world will be driven out" (John 12:32). More about that in the next chapter.

But for now, a final diabological takeaway: we noted above how the grammar of diabolical names—Satan, Beelzebul, and Devil—is weird. Weird in the sense that these names pick out and designate something that is at once singular *and* multiple. Our reflections on exorcism here have drawn into view the idea of an anarchic array of hostile forces which yet have a kind of unity: they are "legion" for they "are many" (Mark 5:9), a marshaled magnitude, the "power of the enemy" (Luke 10:19) and yet the name "Satan" (as we saw) also comprehends the whole.[44] Such observations invite careful reflection on the poetics of such predication. How best to think and speak of this strange unity in diversity of evil, this self-organization of antithetical evil? Should we perhaps speak of it as a diabolical "society" or "system"? As a "corporation" or "corporate person," perhaps *Leviathan*-like?[45] If we do think in such terms, we must be careful to do so in ways that always continue to stress their adventitious and adversarial nature, perhaps by speaking only of "pseudo-persons," "seeming" order, and "parodies" of organization here. Such disciplines of speech would respect the idea that the only thing that actually orders diabolical evil is the contingent shape it assumes in its resistance to and contradicting of the person and work of the Christ as "the Life."

THE CHRISTIAN LIFE: OUR ADVERSARY—RESISTING THE DEVIL

As in the previous chapter, so, too, here allow me by way of concluding reflection to offer two brief observations about the Christian

[44] Cf. Marcus, *Mark 1–8*, 351.

[45] See the famous frontispiece to Thomas Hobbes, *Leviathan*, with its image of "the mortal god." I note Massimo Cacciari's remarks about the way in which the *anomie* of the Enemy is yet a "system" and "order" of energies. Massimo Cacciari, *The Withholding Power: An Essay on Political Theology*, trans. Edi Pucci (Bloomsbury, 2018), 70, 111.

life informed by these reflections on possession and exorcism and envisaged under the promise: "Resist the devil and he will flee" (Jas 4:7). Once again, our first observation concerns the Lord's Prayer.

Prayer for the "coming of God's reign" and the "doing of God's will," as well as the ascription to God of "the kingdom, the power and the glory" all press directly on the business of possession and exorcism we have been exploring. In petitioning for the advent and actualization of the reign of the Lord of Life, we pray for the end of illegitimate dominions, of usurpatious powers, the displacement of everything that illegitimately occupies and preoccupies us and our communities, making for human misery and so dishonoring God. Such prayer seats us inside an eschatological contest of lordships, longing to exchange the deadly and illicit lordship of the adversary for the life-giving reign of Christ. It gives voice to our longing that we be effectively superintended *today* by the love and mercy and justice of the Lord God of Israel that we might know *today* "life in all its fullness" and that the shape of our living might testify to both. To pray for the coming of God's reign is simultaneously to pray for the displacement of those diabolical powers which immiserate the lives of our neighbors, and with them, also our own. As with all prayer, it is the work of the Spirit to hold us responsible for that for which we pray; so, too, here, then, we can find the mainsprings of a Christian ethic committed to resisting the dissolution of life and the depletion of selves and disruption of community that evil brings. This is part of what Barth has in view in describing prayer as the beginning of the Christian's "revolt against disorder," our all-too-human service to the gracious "casting off" and "driving out" of the antithetical power settled and at work in that territory seemingly "held largely by the devil."[46]

The second observation concerns baptism. There is a quite astonishing passage in the article on baptism in the *Belgic Confession* which runs:

> It washes and cleanses from sins and transforms us from being the children of wrath into the children of God. This does not happen by the physical water but by the sprinkling of the precious blood of the Son of God, who is our Red Sea, through which we must pass

[46] Karl Barth, *The Christian Life*, Cornerstones (T&T Clark, 2017), 287.

> to escape the tyranny of Pharaoh, who is the devil, and to enter the spiritual land of Canaan.[47]

The Pharaoh-Devil typology is particularly eye-catching, for it casts the devil not as tempter but as oppressor. The longer Western tradition has considered baptism as a "minor exorcism," something still echoed in Reformed (and other) formularies when baptizands are asked to renounce "the devil and all his works" (or in the newer idiom, "evil and its power in the world"). More important still is how in baptism one owns the death of Christ and shares thereby in the "great exorcism" by which the devil is bound and dispossessed. Conceived in this way, both our sin and our misery under tyranny are the objects of the grace of baptism. As a rite which also signals our inclusion in the community of the church, this practice also loudly echoes the social reintegration of the previously possessed noted above.

A Christian life lived in faithful witness and free obedience to this One will be a life whose passions and actions correspond to God's own passion and action—God's own living and life-giving saving movement—against our misery, and against its deepest and most powerful origins and operations. Baptism attests that one has already been caught up in this divine movement and inaugurates one's own service to counterinsurgency of "The Life" against death and its manifold depletions.

So, to the quite specific form of Christ's victory over diabolical possession there corresponds a militant church which prays for the dispossession of the devil by the coming of the kingdom of God and which baptizes in celebration of the "great exorcism" of the cross, that event in which divine life takes up death for the sake of human life. To seek *this* gift and undertake *this* action is to resist the devil as disciples of One who is "the Life."

CONCLUSIONS AND ANTICIPATIONS

Ernst Käsemann once remarked that "the preaching of the gospel and true discipleship always deal in exorcism. According to the first commandment, it cannot be otherwise. Golgotha makes that evident."[48]

[47] *Belgic Confession* §34, "On Baptism."

[48] Ernst Käsemann, *On Being a Disciple of the Crucified Nazarene*, trans. Roy Harrisville (Eerdmans, 2010), 67.

Just so, it seems. In this chapter we have continued our experiment in thinking theologically about the devil firmly within the bounds of the second article of the creed, and so in close contact and counterpoint to Christ's person and work. Concretely, pursuing this task has meant reflecting upon the evangelical witness to diabolical possession and the work of Jesus Christ as exorcist. We exposited this work as an enactment of his messianic identity as "the Life." Considering possession as an inimical assault upon the good creation that is met and answered by Christ's "driving out" of dissolute powers, we have continued to fill out our negative "portrait in relief" of the devil. The importance of the specifically evangelical setting of possession and exorcism proved decisive. Seen in connection with the advent of the kingdom of God, the agonism of diabolical possession and messianic deliverance acquires a specific, eschatological quality. From this, we also secured some further insight into the Christian life in which prayer for the coming of the kingdom of God and the celebration of the ordinance of baptism draw believers into that movement of the Lord of life which graciously dispossesses death and its proxies.

Jürgen Moltmann once suggested that while Christian theology may not "speak of Satan and daemons in explanatory terms," it can and must speak of the devil in "concrete exorcistic terms." In saying this he seems to have wanted to say that as a positive confession of the God of the gospel, every Christian word and deed always also entails a specific "rejection of the devil and the schemata of this upside-down world."[49] In the language of the *Heidelberg Catechism* we might say that by their faithfulness and freedom, the lives of those who "belong to Christ" and "live for him" serve that great exorcism which has broken the devil's tyranny and thereby celebrate the repossession of the children of God "by his Holy Spirit."

In the next chapter we continue to press forward this experiment in diabology by moving to consider what further purchase we win upon the figure of the devil when we consider diabolical lies and mendacity in connection specifically with the Fourth Gospel's witness to Christ as "the Truth."

[49] Jürgen Moltmann, "Zwölf Bemerkungen zur Symbolik des Bösen," *Evangelische Theologie* 52, no. 1 (1992): 4.

5
DEVILISH LIES— TRUTH'S GAMBIT

While you live, tell truth and shame the devil!

Henry IV, Act III, scene 1

In the last chapter we continued to develop a portrait of the devil as an adversary of Christ by focused consideration of the phenomenon of demonic possession and the exorcisms of Jesus as attested in the Gospels. Possession, I suggested, involved diabolical contradiction of the goodness of creaturely life: "evil spirits" visit misery upon God's children by exploiting human frailties to disrupt and deplete its very forms and functions. Messianic deliverance involved seizing and restoring such depleted lives to the end that they might share in that abundant life which is the *telos* of salvation. The exorcisms of Jesus thus expressed his messianic identity as "the Life" and were seen to form part of a sustained campaign to release women and men out from under the illicit and inhumane influence—indeed, lordship—of these inimical powers. We ended by reflecting briefly on the way such an understanding of possession and exorcism might inflect our understanding of the practice of prayer for the coming of the kingdom of God as well as baptism as forms of "resistance to the devil" in the Christian life.

Our explorations of diabolical temptation and demonic possession in the previous two chapters were focused primarily upon the witness of the Synoptic Gospels. In this present chapter I concentrate attention upon the figure of the devil chiefly as it emerges from the witness of the Fourth Gospel. John the Evangelist's testimony, with its heightened interest in questions of knowledge, truth, and revelation, unfolds the Christian gospel under the proposition that although "no one has ever seen God," the Word made flesh, "the only Son, who is close to the Father's heart" has indeed made God known (John 1:18). The problem animating the Gospel of John, as Marianne Meye Thompson has argued, is the problem of Israel's prophets: namely that "God should be, but is not, known by [God's] people."[1] As the Gospel's prologue has it, though the Word "was in the world, and the world came into being through him; yet the world did not know him. He came to what was his own, and his own people did not accept him" (John 1:10–11). These central themes are then concentrated in Christ's characterization as "the Truth." Exegetical reflections on key Johannine motifs and passages will fix our attention upon the figure of the devil as a "primordial liar" and "ruler" of a world beset by manifold *untruth*, the archenemy of both Truth incarnate and of the Spirit who leads into all truth (John 16:13). I will conclude this chapter once again with some concise discussion of the significance of this for understanding aspects of the Christian life, reflecting upon what it means to pray for forgiveness and for the hallowing of God's name, as well as for the practice of biblical interpretation and proclamation.

THE GOSPEL: ITS ADVERSARY—EXEGETICAL PROVOCATIONS

Unlike the Synoptic Gospels, the Gospel of John includes no temptation story and reports no discrete exorcisms.[2] And yet the Fourth Gospel and associated letters are marked by their own robust diabolical discourse. Our theme is inevitably framed by wider discussions of so-called "Johannine dualism." That concept can be a bit of a blunt

[1] Marianne Meye Thompson, *The God of the Gospel of John* (Eerdmans, 2001), 105; cf. also ch. 3, "The Knowledge of God" as a whole, p. 101ff.

[2] See Ronald A. Piper, "Satan, Demons and the Absence of Exorcisms in the Fourth Gospel," in *Christology, Controversy and Community: New Testament Essays in Honour of David R. Catchpole*, ed. David G. Horrell and Christopher M. Tuckett (Brill, 2000), 253–78.

instrument, used as it is to pick out any number of structuring contrasts in a variety of registers, e.g., metaphysical, ethical, soteriological, etc.[3] Here we use "dualism" as a "flexible trope" to name the role played by oppositional pairs in the complex coding of the Gospel of John and the Johannine Letter corpus.[4]

Scholars will sometimes talk of a "modified dualism,"[5] in part to acknowledge that the key oppositions of light/darkness, above/below, life/death, truth/lies, God/*this* world are fundamental and yet imbalanced in John's witness. They are "imbalanced" because, within the soteriological setting of this Gospel, these oppositions are real and basic yet not permanent in the face of the eschatological victory of Christ toward which events confidently move and in which the negatives are decisively *overcome* (John 16:33).[6] The devil is firmly associated with the negative elements of all these pairs; so also, then, is the

[3] Neil Forsyth, *The Old Enemy: Satan & the Combat Myth* (Princeton University Press, 1987), 299, dates the first use of the term "dualism" in the history of religions to 1700. It is a modern heuristic term. Its meaning and value are also entangled with open debates about the relation of these texts to analogous rhetoric and thoughtforms identified in gnostic and the Qumran communities. For discussion see famously Rudolf Bultmann, *Theology of the New Testament*, vol. 2, trans. K. Grobel (Charles Scribner's Sons, 1955), 15–32; see also Jörg Frey, "Dualism and the World in the Gospel and Letters of John," in *The Oxford Handbook of Johannine Studies*, ed. Judith M. Lieu and Martinus C. de Boer (Oxford University Press, 2016), 274–91; idem, "Recent Perspectives on Johannine Dualism and Its Background," in *Text, Thought, and Practice in Qumran and Early Christianity*, ed. R. Clements and D. R. Schwartz (Brill, 2023), 127–57; John Painter, "Monotheism and Dualism: John and Qumran," in *Theology and Christology in the Fourth Gospel*, ed. G. van Belle et al. (Peeters, 2005), 225–43; Stephen C. Barton, "Johannine Dualism and Contemporary Pluralism," in *The Gospel of John and Christian Theology*, ed. Richard Bauckham and Carl Mosser (Eerdmans, 2008), 3–18; Miroslav Volf, "Johannine Dualism and Contemporary Pluralism," in Bauckham and Mosser, *Gospel of John and Christian Theology*, 19–50.

[4] See Bennie H. Reynolds III, "Demonology and Eschatology in the Oppositional Language of the Johannine Epistles and Jewish Apocalyptic Texts," in *The Jewish Apocalyptic Tradition and the Shaping of New Testament Thought*, ed. Benjamin E. Reynolds and Loren T. Stuckenbruck (Fortress, 2017), 332–33 (327–45).

[5] "In Christianity, on the other hand, the modified dualism of the Testaments of the Twelve Patriarchs achieved a signal triumph, since it offers a simpler and more intelligible solution to the problem of evil than any other ever proposed." W. F. Albright, *From the Stone Age to Christianity*, 2nd ed. (Doubleday/Anchor, 1957), 362. Whether the stated *rationale* here is true is a question.

[6] See Frey, "Recent Perspectives on Johannine Dualism," 149–50.

devil implicated in their eschatological defeat. The diabolical antithesis to God and his Christ in John is at once both absolute *and* passing, implacable *and* destined finally to be overcome. To the Evangelist's confidence in Jesus's certain victory there corresponds a remarkable concentration and intensification of evil. As one commentator observes, "In the fourth gospel all demonism is condensed into the 'Darkness,' the 'World.' There is here a thoroughgoing monism with regard to the activities of evil," which is to say they are all finally one in their singular antithesis to God and God's saving purposes.[7]

Crucially, the cosmic and eschatological idiom of Johannine dualism is overlaid with another, namely, that of the "lawsuit motif." This motif builds upon the legacy of Isaiah 40–55 and casts the ministry of Jesus as an extended "trial" of divine truth and right. Framed in this way, the devil is figured as a subversive antagonist in this contest, a contest in which "the truth of God and God's cause depend upon the truth of Jesus's witness and his cause."[8] In this trial, however, Satan is not a dutiful servant of the court, but rather an anarchic and nihilistic adversary; not a tester of truth but truth's enemy.[9] The truth in question is, of course, finally identified with Christ himself: the one who *is* "the Truth." Questions of disclosure, revelation and "signs," glorification, the effective communication of truth and its reception thus predominate in this telling of the gospel. All this ensures that

7 Anton Fridrichsen, "The Conflict of Jesus with Unclean Spirits," *Churchman* 22, no. 129 (1931): 127 (122–35); repr. in *Exegetical Writings: A Selection*, ed. and trans. Chrys C. Caragounis and Tord Fornberg (Mohr Siebeck, 1994), 71–83. The claim is cited accurately in Trevor Ling, *The Significance of Satan: New Testament Demonology and Its Contemporary Relevance* (SPCK, 1961), 29, though the details of the attribution there are mistaken. Cf. Ernest Haenchen, *John 2: A Commentary on the Gospel of John, Chapters 7–21*, trans. Robert Funk, Hermeneia (Fortress, 1984), 146: "The world is described as darkness" and "the prince of this world is not God but the evil one . . . It is a world remote from God."

8 See Andrew T. Lincoln, *Truth on Trial: The Lawsuit Motif in the Fourth Gospel* (Hendrickson, 2000), 224; cf. 222–24 and 256–62. See also Sigve K. Tonstad, "'The Father of Lies,' 'The Mother of Lies,' and the Death of Jesus (John 12:30–33)," in Bauckham and Mosser, *Gospel of John and Christian Theology*, 193–208. This puts the whole conflict in the register not only of right but also of truth. Indeed, in John the discourse of righteousness is subordinate to that of truth.

9 Such a claim runs against those advanced by others who consider the antagonistic view of Satan an entirely postbiblical development; e.g., Henry Ansgar Kelly, *Satan in the Bible: God's Minister of Justice* (Wipf and Stock, 2017).

the question of the devil and his works is here set in a fundamentally *epistemic* register.

We have already noted the stark Johannine testimony that "the whole world lies in the power of the Evil One" (1 John 5:19). The Fourth Gospel's characterization of "the evil one" as "the ruler (ἄρχων) of this world" is one of its distinctive hallmarks.[10] Under this ruler, the world "presently stands in a state of alienation, and condemnation characterized by darkness, death, sin, slavery and falsehood," and as such is pitched in diametrical opposition to God even as it is also the object of divine saving action.[11] We encounter this ἄρχων at three points across the discourses that make up the central section of the Gospel: first, we read "'Now is the judgment of this world; now *the ruler of this world will be driven out*. And I, when I am lifted up from the earth, will draw all people to myself.' He said this to indicate the kind of death he was to die" (John 12:31–33); next, Jesus relates how he "will no longer talk much with you, for *the ruler of this world is coming*. He has no power over me, but I do as the Father has commanded me, so that the world may know that I love the Father" (John 14:30–31); and finally, Jesus explains how the Spirit, "when he comes, will prove the world wrong about sin and righteousness and judgment: about sin, because they do not believe in me; about righteousness, because I am going to the Father, and you will see me no longer; about judgment, *because the ruler of this world has been condemned*" (John 16:7–11).

The one action to which all three of these sayings relate is, of course, Christ's passion, understood as that event in which the cosmic conflict and trial are resolved, the "hour" of Jesus in which the ruler of this world steps forth, is judged, is condemned, and is driven out.[12]

[10] For discussion of the "ruler of the world" as a Johannine trope see Jutta Leonhardt-Balzer, "The Ruler of the World, Antichrists and Pseudo-Prophets: Johannine Variations on an Apocalyptic Motif," in *John's Gospel and Intimations of Apocalyptic*, ed. Catrin H. Williams and Christopher Rowland (T&T Clark, 2013), 180–99. Interestingly, John never intimates that Satan, the devil, or the *archon* of this world are angels.

[11] D. Moody Smith, *The Theology of the Gospel of John* (Cambridge University Press, 1995), 81, citing John 1:5; 5:19–27; 8:21, 34, 37–44; 12:46. He calls God and world "the primary antipode in the Johannine dualism."

[12] See Gail R. O'Day, "Miracle Discourse and the Gospel of John," in *Miracle Discourse in the New Testament*, ed. Duane F. Watson (SBL, 2012), 188: "In John's gospel, Jesus's power over evil is not localized in any single narrative event like an exorcism

As has been rightly observed: "The hour that brings glory to Jesus brings expulsion to his great enemy."[13] In short, Christ's passion is represented as a single "great exorcism."[14]

For our purposes we note the particular quality of this judgment: what befalls "the ruler of this world" is "not a juridical verdict from on high" but rather "the crushing weight of evidence brought to bear on his person and program by the life and death of the incarnated Logos."[15] When Christ is "lifted up and glorified" on the cross, then the devil is "refuted by the very characteristic of God that he took the lead in denying: truth."[16] The world is reclaimed by its rightful Lord precisely by way of the *truth* of Jesus's case for God and his salvation.[17] The judgment upon "the ruler of this world" is then the judgment of the self-evident truth of cross and resurrection, i.e., the justification of Jesus. In the language of the Johannine Letters, the destruction of the "works of the devil" for which the Son of God comes happens precisely in his *being revealed* (1 John 3:8). The saving victory of Christ is an event of glorification, i.e., an event in which the truth of God is made radiant in the life which the Son lays down and takes up again for the sake of the love of God.[18] What ultimately makes for human freedom and new life is contradiction "from above" of the falsity of the devil's rule, including the misperceptions of God it peddles.[19]

---

prior to the crucifixion. . . . The cosmic battle between good and evil in John will ultimately be resolved only in and through Jesus's hour."

[13] Raymond E. Brown, *The Gospel According to John (I–XII)*, Anchor Bible (Doubleday, 1966), 477.

[14] Richard H. Bell, *Deliver Us from Evil: Interpretating the Redemption from the Power of Satan in New Testament Theology*, WUNT 216 (Mohr Siebeck, 2007), 325–27. I note the phrase "the great exorcism" used again here.

[15] Tonstad, "Father of Lies," 202.

[16] Tonstad, "Father of Lies," 201.

[17] Lincoln, *Truth on Trial*, 216.

[18] Cf. Herman N. Ridderbos, *The Gospel According to John: A Theological Commentary*, trans. John Vriend (Eerdmans, 1997), 438: "Across these chapters the mounting conflict is steadily traced back to the great antithesis in the background of Jesus' coming and work, that of his power struggle with 'the ruler of this world' . . . What is realized in Jesus' glorification as the Son of man . . . is nothing less than the transfer of power over the present God-hating world into the hands of the Son of man. Or, as our text has it, the casting out of this world's ruler."

[19] Tonstad, "Father of Lies," 208: "In the Gospel of John, then, we see Jesus make the ultimate sacrifice in order to put an end to 'the ruler of this world,' understood as

Bultmann saw in all this the existential decision of faith projected and "described in the cosmological terminology of the Gnostic myth," albeit in a somewhat "historicized" form.[20] But I rather think Judith Kovacs is right that the furniture of the Johannine imagination here is more straightforwardly apocalyptic, and that the devil appears neither as "a mere figure of speech," nor a "faded mythological concept," but rather as "an effective power" acknowledged to be "active on the stage of human history."[21] Framed apocalyptically, the career of incarnate Truth in the world is a divine and eschatological judgment (κρίσις), a judgment in which the world's confident "possession" of criteria to discern truth, right, falsehood, and sin is called into question, and its destiny is truly decided.[22]

Now, it is a further distinctive of John's Gospel that "activity that opposes Jesus comes from the devil and is described through the metaphor of parentage" (as with "your father, the devil"; John 8:37–45) and that descriptions of "the *invasive* force of Satan" (as with Judas in John 13:2) as well as the central trope of "the ruler of this world" serve, as we have seen, as "an overarching designation for a power that controls impulses which, on a profound level, contravene what Jesus declares about himself."[23] Our exegetical provocation will not be complete unless and until we confront the chief encounters where this dynamic is at work.

The first case is that of Judas. The Fourth Evangelist writes of how "The devil had already put it into the heart of Judas son of Simon Iscariot to betray him. . . . After he received the piece of bread, Satan entered into him. Jesus said to him, 'Do quickly what you are going to do.' . . . So, after receiving the piece of bread, he immediately went out. And it was night" (John 13:2, 27, 30).

---

the originator of humanity's enduring misperception of God, and to the composite lie that he holds to be its mother."

[20] Rudolf Bultmann, *The Gospel of John: A Commentary*, trans. G. R. Beasley-Murray et al. (Westminster John Knox, 1971), 431.

[21] Judith L. Kovacs, "'Now Shall the Ruler of This World Be Driven Out': Jesus' Death as Cosmic Battle in John 12:2–36," *Journal of Biblical Literature* 114, no. 2 (1995): 228, 234.

[22] See Bultmann, *John*, 564.

[23] Loren Stuckenbruck, "Evil in Johannine and Apocalyptic Perspective: Petition for Protection in John 17," in *John's Gospel and Intimations of Apocalyptic*, ed. Catrin H. Williams and Christopher Rowland (T&T Clark, 2013), 200–232.

Earlier in the Gospel Jesus has already picked out Judas, saying to the disciples that "one of you is a devil" (John 6:70–71). As with Peter's rebuke, so again here: this business of deceitful and intimate betrayal—the betrayal of Jesus into the hands of his enemies to be juridically murdered—*just is* the work of Satan, an outworking of the sheer enmity of the adversary here exercised in and by deceit. Peter's satanic service was temptation; Judas's is betrayal of trust, a deadly and intimate deception. His is a failure to keep faith, a willful decision not to be true. Both the form and the power of Judas's betrayal of Christ is quite properly designated by the Satan's name. As Bultmann comments, "the scene at the last supper in John has the effect of taking the act out of the sphere of human, psychologically-motivated action. It is not a man who is acting here, but Satan himself, the antagonist of God and [of] the Revealer."[24]

The second instance is the fraught exchange between Jesus and "the Jews" with which chapter 8 climaxes. The text reads:

> They answered him, "Abraham is our father." Jesus said to them, "If you were Abraham's children, you would be doing what Abraham did, but now you are trying to kill me, a man who has told you the truth that I heard from God. This is not what Abraham did. You are indeed doing what your father does." They said to him, "We are not illegitimate children; we have one father, God himself." Jesus said to them, "If God were your Father, you would love me, for I came from God and now I am here. I did not come on my own, but he sent me. Why do you not understand what I say? It is because you cannot accept my word. You are from your father the devil, and you choose to do your father's desires. He was a murderer from the beginning and does not stand in the truth because there is no truth in him. When he lies, he speaks according to his own nature, for he is a liar and the father of lies. But because I tell the truth, you do not believe me. Which of you convicts me of sin? If I tell the truth, why do you not believe me? Whoever is from God hears the words of God. The reason you do not hear them is that you are not from God." (John 8:39–47)

Here we meet that "metaphor of parentage" with discomforting forcefulness. Two contextualizing observations: First, this text emerges

[24] Bultmann, *John*, 482. Cf. David Ford, *The Gospel of John: A Theological Commentary* (Baker Academic, 2022), 263–64, who argues for a "multiple realism" here.

from a hot and narrow dispute amongst intimates—a focused family quarrel as it were—fought out in the harsh and "unattractive" rhetoric that marked the most high-stakes arguments of the day: those whose deepest motivations are "of the devil" are here "Jews who *had* believed in him [i.e., Jesus]" (John 8:31).[25] As with Judas, so, too, here: "it is then the breach of faith which betrays Jesus; he who is capable of that is a devil."[26] Second, influential form-critical readings—like those pioneered by J. Louis Martyn—have long suggested that the Gospel as a whole (and texts like this one in particular) constitutes a "two-level drama" in which testimony to Jesus (the *emplotted* meaning) runs parallel with testimony to the conflicted relation between the Johannine community and the contemporary "synagogue" (the *compositional* meaning).[27] So, too, the invective in this exchange is to be contextualized at *both* dramatic levels. Though such contextual observations form part of our own responsible reading, the outsized role of this text in the long history of Christian anti-Judaism must be frankly acknowledged.[28] Indeed, there be no more satanic interpretation of this text than the one which has run rampant through Christian history and

25 See Ruth B. Edwards, *Discovering John: Content, Interpretation, Reception*, 2nd ed. (Eerdmans, 2014), 140.

26 Bultmann, *John*, 451.

27 See J. Louis Martyn, *History and Theology in the Fourth Gospel*, 3rd ed. (Westminster John Knox, 2003) and Raymond E. Brown, *The Community of the Beloved Disciple* (Paulist, 1979). For discussion of debates attending the hypothesis and its implications see Martinus C. de Boer, "The Johannine Community Under Attack in Recent Scholarship," in *The Ways That Often Parted: Essays in Honor of Joel Marcus*, ed. Lori Baron et al. (SBL, 2018), 211–41. One need not discount the rhetorical doubling in order to defend the theological claims as, for instance, does Ridderbos, *Gospel According to John*, 315: "He uses the word [devil] not as invective . . . but to open their eyes to the actual source of their impulses, the real father of their works."

28 The despicable history of Christian antisemitism funded in part by the reception of texts like John 8:44 and the social demonization of the Jews—can there be a more satanic interpretation of this text than that which has run rampant through Christian history? Elaine Pagels's "social history of the devil" suggests that precisely this sociopolitical weaponization of images of "metaphysical evil" is the very point, the original intention of the biblical authors themselves, John included. See Elaine Pagels, *The Origin of Satan* (Random House, 1995), and in closer detail in "The Social History of Satan, the 'Intimate Enemy': A Preliminary Sketch," *Harvard Theological Review* 84 (1991): 105–28, and "The Social History of Satan, Part II: Satan in the New Testament Gospels," *Journal of the American Academy of Religion* 62, no. 1 (1991): 17–58.

helped to fuel the despicable history of Christian antisemitism, a cruel and intimate gentile betrayal of Israel, of the trunk by the ingrafted branches.

It has been observed that when readers dismiss or play down the formative cosmic dualism of the Gospel then they inevitably "make Jesus' human opponents bear the full brunt of [Christ's] indictment."[29] But if we ask the Fourth Gospel why Jesus's opponents fail to acknowledge him and the One who sent him, why they fail to hear the word or "read the signs," and why they fail to maintain their trust and belief in him, then the most definitive and repeated answer this Gospel offers is that they have been kept from doing so by the deceptive arts of the devilish ruler of this world.[30] As one commentator summarizes: "John peers behind the stage of history and sees a mighty malevolent power at work, God's opponent, the devil" and these particular Jewish opponents "have astonishingly become players in a cosmic drama between God and the devil, and they have been enlisted on the wrong side!"[31] This recalls the Gospel's prologue: "He came to his own who received him not." As with Judas, what is at issue here is a betrayal as intimate as it is enigmatic. Both the betrayal and the violence it fuels find their deepest origins and power in the devil, mendacious and murderous "from the beginning," existing and moving outwith and against the truth. While the Johannine Letters will reiterate this under the general rubric of *sin*—"Everyone who commits sin is a child of the devil, for the devil has been sinning from the beginning" (1 John 3:8)—the Fourth Gospel itself puts distinctive and significant emphasis upon *lying*. Raymond Brown comments that for this evangelist, lying "is part of the diabolic realm that is opposed to the truth and light of God. We are not to think here of occasional deception but of fundamental perversion. If Jesus Christ is the truth (John 14:6), the devil is the liar *par excellence* . . . in the Gospel [of John] truth and lying are personified in Jesus and Satan."[32]

[29] Tonstad, "Father of Lies," 207.

[30] See Painter, "Monotheism and Dualism," 242–43.

[31] Henk J. de Jonge, "'The Jews' in the Gospel of John," in *Anti-Judaism and the Fourth Gospel*, ed. R. Bieringer et al. (Westminster John Knox, 2001), 148. For discussion cf. André van Oudtshoorn, "Where Have All the Demons Gone? The Role and Place of the Devil in the Gospel of John," *Neotestamentica* 51, no. 1 (2017): 65–82.

[32] Brown, *Gospel According to John (I–XII)*, 365.

A final word about Pilate to round out these biblical reflections. Close to the heart of John's passion account is Jesus's personal attestation of his mission before Pilate: "For this I was born, and for this I came into the world, to testify to the truth. Everyone who belongs to the truth listens to my voice," and Pilate's famous cynical retort, "What is truth?" (John 18:37–38). Here at the narrative's climax, as in its prologue, the decisive matter of the Gospel is put in the register of truth; and here just as there the one who is the Truth is neither known nor received. Pilate's repudiation of Jesus is distinctive, combining as it does cool abstraction and *Realpolitik* to authorize his dishonesty in handling Jesus. Cowardice and/or calculation fuel betrayal. That Jesus is "handled" in this way shows that falsehood can and does also operate in *this* mode, i.e., by way of a polemical misrelation to the truth, a truth which for the evangelist is of course neither propositional nor referential but finally personal as "revealed in the Incarnation."[33] The scene shows Pilate up as an unwitting child of the "ruler of this world." Perhaps in this he too is paradigmatic of many.

In making the truth that Christ is and the truth that Christ brings its central concern, the Fourth Gospel in turn identifies the devil's chief work to be the generation of unbelief and the cultivation of betrayal: the truth is corroded and obscured in both public and private, in both objective and subjective modes.[34] As directed against Jesus himself—in the figures of Judas, the Jewish detractors, and Pilate—lies and betrayal turn deadly, as Golgotha proves. Thus, the devil is from the beginning a liar *and a murderer.*

THE SAVIOR: HIS ADVERSARY—DIABOLOGICAL RUMINATIONS

These exegetical observations hopefully help us to continue to think of the devil in concrete contact with and contradiction of Jesus the Christ, the One who is "the Way, and *the Truth*, and the Life" (John 14:6a). The devilish work of lying and betrayal is directly at odds with the apocalyptic vocation of the Son to make known the One who sent him and of the Spirit to lead "into all truth." The truth at

33 R. Alan Culpepper, *The Gospel and Letters of John* (Abingdon, 1998), 225.

34 Marianne Meye Thompson, *John: A Commentary*, New Testament Library (Westminster John Knox, 2015), 193. See also Margaret Davies, *Rhetoric and Reference in the Fourth Gospel* (A&C Black, 1992), 157, and Lincoln, *Truth on Trial*, 92.

issue, we have seen, is not so much proposition as it is person. For John's Gospel attests to the person and deeds of Christ as themselves *eloquent*, *radiant*, and—in its own distinctive idiom—*glorious*. If his deeds are in this sense signs—meaning-laden actions freighted with divine communication—so too are Christ's words also deeds: they are effective and authoritative speech able to author and to authorize the life of the children of God (John 1:12). Jesus's speaking and doing up to and including the cross is one sustained campaign of truth undertaken "so that the world may see that he loves the Father, who calls him in the depths of the world and death."[35] It is an extended martyrdom—Truth's gambit, as it were—whose eloquent witness exorcises the deadly falsehoods of the enemy.

As we noted in chapter 2, Augustine is famous for his image of the cross as a "mousetrap" in which, deceptively, the devil is caught. Yet in one of his later sermons he better explains that by the cross "*victus est deceptor*," i.e., "the deceiver was defeated."[36] The devil's deception is not met and overcome by a higher deception but rather by the truth; the devil, we might say, is the Truth's first and only proper *victim*.[37] As we heard from John, the devil does not and cannot "stand in the truth." This same idea of the devil as the proper victim of the Truth of God is expressed in the idea of Christ's passion as "the great exorcism," and is reiterated time and again in the personal decisions of faith: "Whenever someone comes to believe in Christ, the power behind the denial of Christ and God is driven out, which is an exorcism in itself," one commentator explains.[38]

Here again we find a soteriological zero-sum game: the devil's mendacity is strictly inimical to the saving truth of God in Christ. Where the truth of God lovingly comes low in the flesh to enlighten and reveal, it illumines, exposes, and dispels the diabolical night of prevarication, perjury, and prattle, of hypocrisy and haverings.[39] And there are very many modes of opposition and betrayal of the truth:

35 Haenchen, *John 2*, 128.

36 Augustine, Sermon 265D; cited in David Scott-Macnab, "Augustine's Trope of the Crucifixion as a Trap for the Devil and Its Survival in the English Middle Ages," *Viator* 46, no. 3 (2015): 14-15 (1–20).

37 As the Latin *victus* suggests.

38 Leonhardt-Balzer, "Ruler of the World," 199.

39 Bultmann, *John*, 322: Diabolical falsehood, Bultmann says, is essentially marked by "enmity towards the revelation" before going on to explain that "this lying occurs

denial and open contradiction, yes, but also misdirection, suppression, opportune silence, ironizing, trafficking in half-truths. The variety of ways—both objectively and subjectively, knowingly and unknowingly—in which the truth can be undermined, obscured, contradicted, cheapened, etc., are, we might say, *legion*. Moreover, we know, do we not, how invested settled power can be in regimes of untruth. We know too, do we not, how complacent and complicit we too can become with respect to such regimes.[40] Were we honest, we would readily confess that we ourselves are also rather experienced practitioners of these dark, falsifying arts, even if we commonly disassociate them (and our use of them) from any open allegiance with the Old Enemy.

The devil, I say, names the dynamism at work in all the *manifold* possibilities for betraying the truth, that which finds arch expression in the cynicism of Pilate, that which tempts us to despair of truth in the midst of the "hurricane of lies" and betrayals in which so much of life—spiritual, political, economic, personal—seems to move and (almost) have its being.[41] Indeed, we might take the corrosion of confidence in truth and honesty as such to be a diabolical ambition. As Susan Neiman remarks: "evil is not merely the opposite of good but inimical to it. True evil aims at destroying moral distinctions themselves."[42] What is said here of the good certainly holds also for the true: demonic evil works to deprive us not only of truth but also of the conditions of possibility for discerning the truth. It also rhymes perfectly with the dynamic power of falsehood and intimate betrayal

---

in everything women and men say and do in resistance to the revelation which encounters them."

[40] For those of us of a certain age, the witness of Eastern European dissidents like Václav Havel and Jan Patočka and their seemingly mundane concept of "living in truth" as the condition of possibility and mainspring of authentic political life and service comes to mind in this connection. See Václav Havel, *Living in Truth*, ed. Jan Vladislav (Faber & Faber, 1986) and "The Power of the Powerless," in *Open Letters: Selected Writings, 1965–1990*, ed. Paul Wilson (Knopf, 1991), 125–214; together with Jan Patočka, *The Selected Writings of Jan Patočka: Care for the Soul*, ed. Ivan Chvatník and Erin Plunkett, trans. Alex Zucker (Bloomsbury, 2022), 18 (for example).

[41] The phrase "hurricane of . . . lies" is taken from Green Day's rock opera, *American Idiot* (2004), as angry, nearly prophetic, and wearingly pertinent a lyrical castigation of the social and human consequences of the loss of confidence in the possibility of truth and honesty in personal and public life as one might find.

[42] Susan Neiman, *Evil in Modern Thought* (Princeton University Press, 2002), 287.

which the Fourth Gospel grounds in the antithetical operations of the "ruler of this world."

Crucially, it seems to me, diabolical falsehood and lying keeps close company with the problem of idolatry. For the problem of idolatry is the problem of *false* gods—of "so-called gods" or "gods who are no gods" as Paul has it (1 Cor 8:4–5)—and also of the *false* worship of the true God. The problem of idolatry, then, is precisely the problem of discerning and recognizing what is true in the midst of the flurry of the *ersatz*, the simulacrum, the virtual, the pseudo-, the imitation, the merely "god-like," the divine-*ish*. As idolators discover, our betrayal of the truth here is soon enough returned in kind, as the idol itself inevitably betrays our trust in turn. Perhaps the worry about idolatry is so sharp precisely because, as the gospel reminds us, "hostility to revelation is as such hostility to life."[43]

Two more directly diabological observations if I may. First, in an echo of the odd "collective" nature of Satan noted in our discussion of exorcism in the previous lecture, so, too, here, we note how designations of the devil as "the ruler of this world" and "father of lies" function as a kind of collective name for all that concentrates and funds the manifold misconstruals and contradictions of the truth of the God of the gospel.[44] The devil "appears" in our disbelief and betrayal as its underlying ground and source, as it were. As one commentator remarks, in John "one can still speak of the ruler of this world, to be sure, but that ruler does not put in an appearance himself . . . the world that is hostile to Christ and inimical to God is represented only by human disbelief."[45] David Ford in his recent commentary finds the impulse to demythologize at this point irresistible, explaining that

[43] Bultmann, *John*, 321.

[44] Jan G. van der Watt, "Salvation in the Gospel According to John," in *Salvation in the New Testament: Perspectives on Soteriology*, ed. H. J. Bernard Combrink and Jan G. van der Watt (Brill, 2005), 118: "The devil is, however, described as the father of unbelievers and a prince of this world . . . both social terms indicating group orientation. In all three contexts where the devil is called the prince of this world, the dominating themes are the victory of Jesus over this prince through the cross-events and the consequent powerlessness and the presence of judgement over this prince and everything that belongs to him. What are the soteriological implications? By overpowering this father and prince, Jesus actually overpowers his whole family and group . . ."

[45] Haenchen, *John 2*, 30–31.

"evil is personified in Satan, but he is not a full character in the drama. He represents murder, lies, betrayal, and the violation of trust and love. Those powerful dynamics of 'this world.'"[46] That the devil is an odd kind of character is certainly true. That this suggests a merely literary "representation" of purely human machinations—for the evangelist and/or for our theology—I am not so certain.

Second, we pause over the claims in John 8:44 that when the devil lies "he speaks *according to his own nature* (ἐκ τῶν ἰδίων λαλεῖ) for he *is* a liar and the father of lies," and that the devil *is* one "in whom there is no truth." Taken together, these claims are as close to a metaphysical definition of the being of the devil as we have yet come across. Diabolical enmity to truth goes deep, indeed all the way down—it is congenital, constitutional. To be the devil is to be incapable of truth; divine truth and diabolical being are mutually exclusive. One could say that the devil is entirely and exhaustively identified with his trade. The adversary's mendacity and the violence which accompanies it would seem then to be "of the very nature of the Devil."[47] This comports with the recurrent Johannine emphasis that his mendacity, murderousness, and sinfulness are each and all "*from the beginning*," a turn of phrase not to be overinterpreted, but which strongly suggests originary identity.[48] The strictly *adversarial* quality of the devil thus receives strong affirmation and specification here. It is true that the question of the origin of the "ruler of this world" and of "the darkness" is not properly asked or answered here: evangelical interest is and remains, I think, exhausted in the devil's present conflict with Christ and defeat in his glorification of God.[49] But it is also true, as

46 Ford, *Gospel of John*, 264.

47 Bultmann, *John*, 321. Cf. Ridderbos, *Gospel According to John*, 315: "His speech is by definition false. For his name is 'liar,' and he is the father of falsehood. In that connection one must not just think of dishonesty or mendacity in a moral sense, for the lie here is the antithesis of what in v. 32 is called the truth."

48 Theological commentators on these verses in John's Gospel and the Johannine Letters regularly lead with cautionary denials of metaphysical dualism and/or Manichaeism before remarking further. See Calvin's commentaries, for example.

49 Painter, "Monotheism and Dualism," 237. David Ford argues that John shows no "independent interest in this figure's person, origins, or future" but is keen to motivate confidence in face of its power as it wins power only if "feared," if its "falsehoods are believed and trusted . . . and obeyed." Ford, *Gospel of John*, 245.

regards the question of origin, that nowhere in the Johannine corpus is the devil identified as an angel.

As these remarks make plain, I think, while it brings out its own distinctive emphases to be sure, specific consideration of the devil in contradiction to Jesus Christ as "the Truth" also in effect reprises our previous considerations of the devil as the adversary of Christ as both "Way" and "Life." To speak of Christ as Truth is in a sense to revisit these identity descriptions in another, epistemic register. Or perhaps better, it is to consider the clarity and effectiveness of claims made about Christ as "the Way" and "the Life." So, too, have our remarks about the devil here in part reprised themes first met in considering temptation and possession, since the deadly falsehood of the devil specifies the means and power by which those inimical assaults against God's Messiah and God's good creature are prosecuted.

THE CHRISTIAN LIFE: OUR ADVERSARY—RESISTING THE DEVIL

As with the two previous chapters, we end this present chapter with two brief observations about the bearing all this might have upon our understanding of the Christian life as life under the promise: "Resist the devil, and he will flee" (Jas 4:7). The first concerns the Lord's Prayer.

We recall once more that prayer is an act of faithfulness and service which—by grace and the Spirit—answers humanly to the faithfulness and service of the Savior. Accounting for diabolical falsehood as we have presses upon what it means for the Christian community to pray that God's "name be hallowed" and indeed for the "forgiveness of sins." In both petitions we seek from the Lord the grace to stand in truth, to be "of the truth," and to live from truth. In doing so we ask, in the first petition, to have our idolatry brought to light so that we might untangle ourselves from our false gods and false worship of the true God. "Hallowing" here is thus not merely a linguistic discipline, but rather something much more comprehensive, comprising the entire way in which one lives before and speaks to and of *Hashem*, "the Name." This, I think, is what the Fourth Gospel calls "doing what is true" (John 3:21). This prayer leads us to consider and take renewed responsibility for the "truth" of our relation to God, its aptness, fittingness, and correspondence. To ask the Lord for forgiveness as we do in the other petition is to ask to have our lives truly illumined in a way that we simply cannot bring about ourselves. In part what we seek is liberation from the self-deception that drives both our self-justification as well as our misunderstanding and mistreatment of neighbors. Alert to the depth of diabolical delusion and the manifold forms of deception which beset us, we can and must pray for the kind of *insight* and *honesty* only God can give. The forgiveness of sin, for us and for others, and the freedom it brings in its train has the divine gift of truth and truthfulness as its origin and mainspring.

In Christ, true humanity joins true divinity in the struggle against the depths of dishonesty and distrust which assaults truth and corrodes our faith in it. A Christian life lived in faithful witness and free obedience to this One who is the Truth will be a life whose passions and actions correspond to God's own passion and action—God's own saving movement—against falsehood, bad faith, dishonesty, and betrayal. We might think of such a life as *parabolic life*, i.e., the discerning enactment of true, human parables of the reign of God, an adventurous inhabitation of forms of life that "tell the truth" about what they owe to the gospel and its "great exorcism" of the deceptive and deadly power at work in the powers of this world.

The second observation concerns the interpretation of Scripture and the practice of preaching, both activities indexed to the truth. The reading of Scripture and the act of preaching take place in the midst of the economy of salvation, and we owe ourselves a properly theological description of these acts and their location.[50] What if our account of that saving economy were to include acknowledgment of the reality of diabolical distortion and deception as regards the truth—and most especially the truth of the gospel itself? What if we let the figures of Peter and Judas remind us that the most satanic betrayal of the truth is its most intimate betrayal, i.e., its betrayal by those called by, drawn to, and formed by it? We have already seen that the devil *qua* hermeneut and rhetor can and does cite Scripture to good effect in his campaign against "the Way." The words themselves are no talisman against their antithetical deployment; the affordances of the text are, we dare say, *legion* and not at all harmless. Is

[50] For two different examples of such theological description of Scripture within the economy of salvation see the treatments in John Webster, *Holy Scripture: A Dogmatic Sketch* (Cambridge University Press, 2003) and Katherine Sonderegger, *Systematic Theology I: The Doctrine of God* (Fortress, 2015).

there any text which could not in some way be sharpened into a "text of terror" and wielded as such in our preaching and teaching?

To acknowledge that devilish falsehood besets even—and especially—our encounters with Scripture requires us to make *critical* hermeneutics a work entirely proper to faith and theology. Exegesis is itself a site where the struggle of truth and falsehood is fundamentally enjoined, where interpretation is fraught with peril. Is our reading of the gospel actually a reading *of the gospel*? Is our reading of the gospel of God actually *of God*? Our struggle with Satan at this juncture becomes, I suggest, crucially and unavoidably material, i.e., *sachkritische*. Yet, to see our reading of Scripture exposed to diabolical mendacity is finally to confess that our exegetical devices, hermeneutical strategies, and our wiles as interpreters cannot in and of themselves ensure the truth; we do not possess infallible truth procedures. Our methods, as Hanna Reichel has recently reminded us theologians, cannot save us.[51] Life with Scripture and its expression in preaching can only be risked: a humble adventure of faith in the One who has promised to lead us into all truth.

To the quite specific form of Christ's victory over diabolical lying, there corresponds a militant church which prays that God's name be hallowed and for its sins to be forgiven, a church which remembers in its reading and preaching of Scripture that it must ever be "led into Truth" by Son and Spirit. To seek *this* gift and undertake *this* action is to resist the devil, the "father of lies," as disciples of the Truth.

CONCLUSIONS AND ANTICIPATIONS

In this, the penultimate chapter of this study, I have endeavored to augment and sharpen our theological portrait of the devil by espying him in relief—backlit, as it were—by the light of Christ who is "the Truth," whose way and life for us are true, a glorification of the One who sent him. The Fourth Gospel expresses the fundamental antagonism of Christ and devil firmly in the register of truth. The quality and depth of the devil's enmity to the God of the gospel and the gospel of God finds acute expression in his characterization as a liar, murderer, and sinner "from the first." The saving movement of Christ as Truth brought to light the reality of "this world" as one captive to

[51] Hanna Reichel, *After Method: Queer Grace, Conceptual Design, and the Possibility of Theology* (Westminster John Knox, 2023).

and possessed by manifold diabolical falsehoods and betrayals, and yet also at the same time the object of "the great exorcism" of Christ's passion. From it, we also won some insights into the Christian life as life marked by prayer for the hallowing of God's name and the forgiveness of sin, as well as placing the struggles which attend the interpretation and preaching of Scripture in the struggle for freedom from entanglement in the deceptions of the adversary.

In the final chapter to come I hope to gather up insights drawn together from across these three concise experiments in biblical-theological diabology, and to return once more to the ponder questions of the place, function, and substance of the "devil in our doctrine."

6
THE DEVIL IN OUR DOCTRINE

> For Jesus Christ worked against the devil, and destroyed his power over hearts (of which exorcism is the figure) to establish the Kingdom of God.[1]
>
> Pascal

To open this concluding chapter, let me rehearse briefly the path we have been following and which has led us here. After first attempting to motivate interest in the devil as a theme for Reformed theology on cultural, ecumenical, and biblical grounds in the introductory chapter, I then moved in a second chapter to sketch something of the career of the devil in Christian theology in the West. There I set out the "majority report," which from the time of Augustine up into the modern period fixed the default dogmatic location of diabology firmly within the first article of the creed and its fundamental framing doctrines—namely, angelology, privative evil, and providence—and established its recurrent preoccupations, i.e., refuting dualism, refusing moral exculpation for sin, etc. Effectively isolated both formally and materially from the matter of salvation in this way, and under

[1] "Car Jésus-Christ agissait contre le diable et détruisait son empire sur les cœurs, dont l'exorcisme est la figuration, pour établir le royaume de Dieu." Blaise Pascal, *Pensées* #820, ed. Léon Brunschvicg (Gallimard, 1897).

pressures both rational and exegetical, the doctrine finally "gave way" for many in the modern period, having proved itself to be but an unnecessary and troublesome legacy. I suggested, however, that there were also intimations in the tradition of another approach to the doctrine—visible, for example, in some of the early and formative catechetical texts of the Reformed churches and gestured at by Karl Barth's twentieth-century account of "nothingness"—an approach which would place the devil close to the heart of the doctrine of salvation, and so connect it first and foremost with the substance of the concerns of the second article of the creed. Associating myself with this minority report, I then proposed to undertake a little experiment in alternative diabology.

The three central chapters of this study just concluded went in search of the devil anew, as it were. Espying him in particular upon the pages of the Gospels, we met and contemplated him there as the "worker of his inimical works," the stubborn antagonist of the Christ. These chapters endeavored to build up a profile of the devil "in negative relief" by attending to the specific form and dynamism this enmity assumed in its opposition to the saving work and person Christ attested as "the Way, and the Life, and the Truth." This threefold characterization of Christ organized matters and in turn illumined a threefold antagonism to the work of saving grace made concretely manifest in diabolical temptation, demonic possession, and devilish deceit. In this way we contemplated what Joseph Ratzinger once aptly described as "the extreme crystallization of the demonic" precisely in contrast to the figure of Christ.[2] Questions of the identity, agency, and ontology of the devil have been broached along the way, and I suggested that descriptions like *adventitious*, *adversarial*, and *anarchistic* afforded some purchase upon the devil's rather peculiar figure—more about these matters in a moment. Each of these three central chapters also touched briefly upon some ways in which our thinking about the devil in this way provided new and interesting perspectives upon aspects of the prayer and practices of the Christian life, now made visible in new ways as varied forms of faithful resistance to diabolical enmity to Christ, both without and within the Christian community. The ambition throughout in approaching

[2] Joseph Ratzinger, "Farewell to the Devil?" in *Dogma and Preaching*, ed. Michael J. Miller, trans. Michael J. Miller and Matthew J. O'Connell (Ignatius, 2011), 200.

matters in this way has been to expose our thinking on this awkward subject once again to the lively biblical testimony from which it fundamentally derives. For any Reformed theological treatment of this theme, I would argue, must ultimately involve taking renewed dogmatic responsibility in the present for the substance, form, force, and entailments of this testimony.

In this concluding chapter, then, I want to consider directly some theological "matters arising" from all this and to venture some claims about "the devil in our doctrine." These claims must be fitted to the nature of our experiment and its brevity: none are hard deductions, most will take the form of summary restatements, conceptual inferences, and inductive developments. Though expressed as propositions, the tone throughout will of necessity be tentative, the mood frequently subjunctive. Even as one tries to draw together claims and trace implications, I offer only "sketches" of what might be involved in well-ordered Christian thought and speech in this quarter rather than offer up any "system."[3] For we are, after all, confronting a double mystery here, for we are reflecting upon the *mysterium iniquitatis* (2 Thess 2:7) from within the *mysterium Evangelii* (Eph 6:19). Not only that, but in this matter, confident conceptual solutions are perhaps particularly misplaced. As Donald MacKinnon usefully reminds us:

> It is a lesson to be learnt from tragedy that there is no solution to the problem of evil; it is a lesson which Christian faith abundantly confirms, even while it transforms the teaching by indication of its central mystery. In the Cross the conflicting claims of truth and mercy are reconciled by deed and not by word. The manner of their reconciliation is something which lies beyond the frontier of our comprehension; we can only describe and redescribe.[4]

When B. B. Warfield—the patron of the lectureship from which this book derives—sought to "describe and redescribe" Christ's saving act on the cross, he quite properly emphasized both its *divine* quality as

3 In this commitment to offering a theological "sketch," I share the sensibility concerning the nature of this kind of theological writing expressed by Paul J. Griffiths and performed persuasively in his study *Israel: A Christian Grammar* (Fortress, 2023), xiii, 10, *passim*.

4 Donald M. MacKinnon, "Atonement and Tragedy," in *Borderlands of Theology and Other Essays*, ed. George W. Roberts and Donovan E. Smucker (Lutterworth, 1968), 104.

well as its *costliness*.[5] In "describing and redescribing" that same saving act with specific reference to the devil, this short study has called particular attention to its *agonistic* and *redemptive* quality, and thus encouraged us to think a little differently about the truth and mercy of God enacted in Jesus Christ. We have in a way been asking how these might appear when we firmly acknowledge, as Emil Brunner once wrote, that in the New Testament witness the background provided by "the existence of the powers of darkness (however this may be conceived)—is integral to the story of Jesus Christ."[6]

SOME DOGMATIC THESES ABOUT THE DEVIL

Already with such remarks we have begun to take stock of something of the theological "yield" of our experimental reconsideration of the figure of the devil with firm and consistent reference to the person and work of the Savior. Allow me to try to order my further remarks and sketch of this "yield" around four themes: (1) the dogmatic location of the devil, (2) the priority of redemption in soteriology, (3) diabolical identity, being, and act, and (4) discipleship in the face of the adversary.

§1 Dogmatic location and ordering

Our first claim is that, dogmatically, Christian teaching concerning the devil best belongs to the doctrines of the second article of the creed. The dramatic role of the devil is, we might say, expressed with maximum compression when the Apostles' Creed says that Jesus "suffered" (*passus* / παθόντα). The whole course of Christ's life and ministry—everything which he underwent between his birth and his death *sub Pontio Pilato*—is there encompassed and included. Without excluding "suffering" in the narrower sense, the meaning of the term is more capacious, meaning all that Jesus "underwent" or "endured." We have attended to the ways in which the confrontation with the devil as tempter, usurper, and liar is integral to the Gospels' telling of the way of the Messiah to the cross. We have seen how *this* confrontation and struggle is ingredient in his activity and identity as Savior:

5 Benjamin Breckinridge Warfield, "The New Testament Terminology of 'Redemption,'" in *Biblical Doctrines*, vol. 2 of *The Works of Benjamin B. Warfield* (repr., Baker Book House, 1981), 327–74.

6 Emil Brunner, *The Christian Doctrine of Creation and Redemption*, trans. Olive Wyon (Lutterworth, 1952), 134.

he is Christ Jesus *agonistes*. The testimony to the Savior's life and work set forth in the Gospels presents us with a three-agent drama from start to finish. We meet the devil in that drama. We meet the devil there as the great antagonist of everything Christ purposes and achieves. Is it too much to say that the devil is ingredient in the telling of the gospel of salvation as we receive it from the apostolic witness? Is it possible to register the true goodness of the good news of the gospel of God, apart from recognition of this?

In the account I am proposing the devil does not appear in the beginning but in the middle. The devil makes his evangelical appearance *in medias res*. We come to speak of the devil here in giving an account of the actual state of affairs which the saving advent of Christ brings to light. Walter Sparn is thus right to say that Christian talk of the devil becomes meaningful only within the horizon provided by proclamation of the gospel of salvation.[7] But we can be more precise: the devil appears as a topic in and belongs to our contemplation of the outworking of salvation in virtue of what Calvin called "the whole course of Christ's obedience."[8] This is its native province. Soteriology is the dogmatic locus where it proves both concrete and consequential. A crucial feature of this soteriological framing is a recognition that the profile of the devil takes shape and is glimpsed only in its specific and proximate contact with Christ. The devil is manifest first and foremost as "anti-Christ," the enemy and opponent of the saving transit of the One who is truly God and truly human, the one who comes low "for us and for salvation." The gospel, I suggest, has a derivative but real interest in the devil: "derivative" because it meets and thinks of the devil solely as Christ's *adversary*; "real" because the shape and substance of its primitive testimony suggests that good news cannot be rightly heard and understood without it.[9]

[7] Walter Sparn, "Über den Teufel," in *Religion in Geschichte und Gegenwart*, 4th ed., ed. Hans Dieter Betz et al. (Mohr Siebeck, 2007), s.v.: "Der Sinnhorizont christlichen Redens vom Teufel is daher die Verkündigung des Evangeliums."

[8] John Calvin, *Institutes of the Christian Religion* (1559), trans. Ford Lewis Battles (Westminster, 1960), 2.16.5. Calvin takes the Apostles' Creed to state "the leading articles of redemption in a few words, and may thus serve as a tablet in which the points of Christian doctrine, most deserving of attention, are brought separately and distinctly before us." *Institutes* 2.16.18.

[9] James Kallas, *The Significance of the Synoptic Miracles* (SPCK, 1961), 107: New Testament "eschatology cannot be understood apart from demonology."

Reformed theologians—but not only them—should, I think, be ambitious for our theological thinking to share this "biblical attitude" toward the devil.[10] One could do this in a variety of ways, to be sure. But I would suggest that rehousing the devil in the second article of the creed, and so taking Christology and soteriology as its most proper and determinative dogmatic location, should be one defining mark of any such attempt. This is to say that the fundamental shape and function of theological talk of the devil ought to be determined primarily in that dogmatic locus, with questions connected to other aspects of doctrine—like first article concerns about creation and providence, etc.—deferred and sub-ordered accordingly. Housed in the first article, the devil is readily and safely domesticated, a tethered rebel angel in the service of the outworking of providence. Housed in the second article, the devil is met and confronted as feral evil, the vicious, intimate, and intractable enemy of God, God's Christ, and God's good creatures.

§2 The encompassing priority of redemption

Our second claim follows from the first: when we acknowledge that the devil as Christ's adversary is a prominent and ubiquitous ingredient in the evangelical testimony to the outworking of salvation, then our understanding of the form and substance of that salvation itself is affected. I agree with the Swiss theologian Henry Mottu that the controlling concern of all Christian theology is "Jesus Christ, his work and person, as the polemical encounter of God's reality with the reality of the world."[11] Mottu takes the term "polemical" from Bonhoeffer, who in his *Ethics* describes the achievement of salvation as the realization of a living and "polemical unity" between God and the world God comes to save.[12] This talk of salvation in the language

[10] Karl Barth spoke of seeking to win a "biblical attitude" (*eine biblische Haltung*) in theology, i.e., aspiring to a "fundamental uniformity between the mindset of the biblical writers—including the way in which questions are asked and answered by them—and that of the church's preachers and dogmaticians." *Church Dogmatics* I/2, 816–17 (translation altered). Dogmatics can best do so by remaining in "constant contact" with exegesis, laboring to "acquire this determinate form of thought only in confrontation with the biblical text." *Church Dogmatics* I/2, 822 (translation altered). I concur.

[11] Henry Mottu, "Bonhoeffer and Our Theological Existence Today," in *A Bonhoeffer Legacy*, ed. A. J. Klassen (Eerdmans, 1981), 210.

[12] See Dietrich Bonhoeffer, *Ethics*, vol. 6 of *Dietrich Bonhoeffer Works*, ed. Clifford Green, trans. Richard Krauss et al. (Fortress, 2005), 59.

of polemics injects a valuable agonistic note into the concept of reconciliation, reminding us that reconciliation involves judgment and forgiveness, i.e., that God moves *against* sin for the sake of righteousness and the rectification of the world.

But our reflections on the devil in this "brief theology" provide an even more expansive and necessary gloss upon the meaning of the word "polemical" in Mottu's proposition. As we have seen, Christ's saving confrontation with the devil as tempter, usurper, and liar has the form of a sustained *polemos* with *this* world and the "ruler of *this* world" precisely for the sake of the world. As one of our poets observes, "the whole Christian message is permeated with the urgency of rescue."[13] As has emerged with particular sharpness from our reflections on possession and exorcism, both human misery and human transgressions, both the depletion of human selfhood as well as its titanic inflation are the object of divine salvation in Christ. Our thinking about the devil has helped to bring this "full-orbed" account of the saving work of Christ back into view.

But what has come back into view is not just a full-orbed account but also a *reordered* one. Thinking again about the devil as we have here, I believe, pushes us to acknowledge the priority of redemption over reconciliation in our soteriological doctrine.[14] This work of salvation is *principally* a work of deliverance, of redemption, of liberation. For Christ as "the Way" to resist temptation in order to walk the Way of the Cross as the path of the Messiah, for Christ as "the Life" to deliver and repossess the possessed for the sake of life and "life abundant," and for Christ as "the Truth" to defeat falsehood and betrayal by the enactment of divine and human truth and to dispel darkness by the advent of light—these are each and together visions of redemption prosecuted on behalf of a world captive to illicit and oppressive powers, a world whose time and space and sociality are diabolically organized by doubt, death, and lies. The problem of reconciliation and forgiveness is properly nested within the more encompassing concern for redemption: for it is those who are rescued

[13] Jack Clemo, *The Invading Gospel: A Return to Faith* (Marshall Pickering, 1986), 91–92.

[14] I have discussed this question of the sequencing of soteriological concerns elsewhere; see "Christ Must Reign: The Priority of Redemption," in *Militant Grace: The Apocalyptic Turn and the Future of Christian Theology* (Baker Academic, 2018), 53–70.

from the oppressive captivity to powers too strong for us to throw off who are then, in freedom, also confronted with their complicity and all too willing service to those very captivating powers. Reflecting upon the devil evangelically as we have sets this dynamic of captivity and complicity before us in a comprehensive, cosmic register; but we can recognize it also as it repeats itself severally in social and political and psychological registers as well.

Tarrying with the devil as we have in these few pages has reminded us not only of the redemptive nature of our salvation but also the *depth* and *breadth* of the problem to which salvation in Christ is the solution. When we think as we must in Christian soteriology back from solution to plight, from the quality of God's saving action in Christ back to the quality of the captivity from which it secures release, then we are led to acknowledge the radicality of that captivity and the terrible "strength" of our captor(s). We are reminded that salvation is addressed to both our expansive malfeasance and the depth of our misery. The devil figures, as we have stressed, first and foremost as "*God's* adversary" in Christ and because God's adversary, then also as ours. Perhaps, as Isaak Dorner observes, one of the tasks of the devil in our doctrine is to supply an account of the nature and power of evil which respects precisely this hard soteriological realism and "resists volatilization."[15]

Finally, having motivated these judgments almost exclusively from theological reflection on the four gospels as we have, we might also note at this juncture that the "three-agent drama" of salvation—a redemptive contest involving God, the human, and the anti-God power(s)—proves not to be an idiosyncratic feature merely of the Apostle Paul's apocalyptic theology. Rather, the "exchange of lordships," which according to Käsemann is the hallmark of Pauline soteriology, keeps very close company with the redemptive vision in all four Gospels which attest the work of the cross to be a "great exorcism" by means of which the insurgent "ruler of *this* world" is driven out by the Lord. We may also recall here that the great deliverance of Israel out of Egypt which is the paradigm of redemption is itself scripted as a "three-agent drama"—something we saw reflected in the

[15] Isaak A. Dorner, *A System of Christian Doctrine*, vol. 3, trans. Alfred Cave and J. S. Banks (T&T Clark, 1885), 108.

Belgic Confession when it drew parallels between Pharaoh and the devil in relation to the meaning of baptism.

This last observation may in fact provide a key to the wider question about the connection of our theme to the witness of the Old Testament. It seems to me that it is the exodus as both prototype and archetype of the three-agent drama of redemption, together with Israel's heated polemics against idolatry—especially when directed inward—that are more immediately salient to a Christian doctrine of the devil than are the few and isolated appearances of talk of "*the satan*" in the Old Testament texts. I would suggest that it is in the former rather than the latter that we properly meet and learn the biblical grammar of redemption and within it that of the adversary. If the "Jobian Satan" provides the archetype and model of the devil found in the doctrine of the traditional "majority report" I traced in chapter 2, then the Pharaoh of Exodus might be said to provide that attested and preserved in the parallel "minority report" with which we have been experimenting here. In short: it must be Egypt's divine Pharaoh, and not the heavenly courtier of the book of Job, who provides the true and best type of which the devil of the Gospels is antitype. Intuitions of this appear in the archive of Christian faith and thought, of course, and it would be good and useful to excavate them fully in the service of recalling the Christian mind to reckon with the devil who "rules over the great Egypt of the world," as one ancient theologian put it suggestively.[16]

§3 Diabolical identity, agency, and ontology

Over the course of this study we have commented in passing about the identity, agency, and ontology of the devil, and it would be useful to try to consolidate what can be said here.

The majority tradition, you will recall, answered these kinds of questions quite handily out of the first article of the creed: the devil is a creature, an angelic creature, who, though fallen, "is" yet an angel, retaining the nature and natural powers of just such a creature; the privative nature of evil secures this point. The actions of such a fallen angel are and remain "angelic" in form (hence spiritual, rational, nondiscursive, without physical body) and force (hence, preternatural if

[16] Methodius, *The Symposium* 4.2, trans. Herbert Musurillo (Longman, Green and Co., 1958), and also at 76, where we also read: "Pharaoh was a type of the devil."

not supernatural). The devil's willful fall, of course, irrevocably disorders all this as to its desires and ends, including its ultimate end in God. But the devil is not *identical* with evil, nor as creature could he be understood to become evil *without remainder*. All this casts the devil rather as *the* rebellious creature of rebellious creatures, a first among many, the captain of sinners. Within the architecture of the doctrine of creation it was possible for the tradition to say quite a bit about the identity, agency, and ontology of the devil and do so with fair confidence because it had quite a bit to say about angels, having the confidence of its exegesis (of the angelic fall) and of its metaphysics (angelic and otherwise).

But what of the scope for addressing these same topics within the "minority report"? Having tethered our thinking firmly in the second article and approached the devil with a keen interest chiefly in his antagonistic contravention of the work of Christ, just what might we be able to say of these things? Perhaps not nearly so much and that perhaps also without the confidence that has marked the tradition. Nevertheless, as has been suggested at points along the way, I want to suggest that the quality of the devil's being and agency might responsibly be characterized chiefly as *adversarial*, *adventitious*, and *anarchic*. Let me offer a little more by way of explication of each.

By *adversarial*, I mean to signal that the being of the devil "is" and "is what it is" exclusively in virtue of its antithesis and contradiction of God and God's good purposes and acts. The devil *is* only because and as he is *against* God, lacking independent positive existence or grounds for existence. His is a being that is entirely exhausted in its negative actions, i.e., temptation, possession, dissimulation, and betrayal. As the Fourth Gospel has it, "The thief comes *only* to steal and kill and destroy" (John 10:10).[17] The intuition here is that what the privation account of evil has always said about evil—that it is without positive being, that it "is" only in its contradiction of being, etc.—can and should be said about the devil as such; that the interval

[17] Thomas F. Torrance, *The Christian Doctrine of God: One Being Three Persons* (T&T Clark, 2016), 227: "It is a virulent, demonic force radically antagonistic to all that is holy and orderly, right and good . . . more than the hypostatisation of a principle of contradiction between God and the world. . . . [It is] in fact an organized kingdom of evil and darkness with a kind of headquarters of its own . . ."

between evil and the devil should be completely closed. Implicit in such a view is the claim that the figure of the devil is not properly conceived as a creature, angelic or otherwise.

The term *adventitious* intends to bring precisely this claim to expression. For it signals that the devil has no *proper* place in either the creation or new creation, but is ontologically incidental and alien, appearing only ever as an entirely extraneous factor, something insubstantial yet actual, something that ought not to be, yet is. In talking this way I have begun to avail myself of paradoxical forms of speech not unlike Barth's talk of sin and evil and "nothingness" (*das Nichtige*) as an "impossible possibility" or as a factor "impossible yet actual" and his difficult assertion cited earlier that "demonic action has no ontology."[18] Pseudo-Dionysius once asserted that evil is "not among the things that have being, nor is among what is not in being" before going on to specify that "it has a greater nonexistence and otherness from the Good than nonbeing has."[19] To think of the reality of the devil as one marked by that "far greater nonexistence and otherness" is, I think, precisely the challenge. Just what I am here calling the adventitious quality of diabolical reality is what such awkward forms of speech are intended to pick out. They are ways of gesturing at the weird ontological status of this antithetical power, its being neither God nor creature, yet "being" still, its "being" only in its virulent annihilating relation to what is. Perhaps Paul's talk of the anti-God powers as "so-called gods"—who are "by nature not gods" and yet still exercise actual power to subjugate (1 Cor 8:5; Gal 4:8)—points at the same puzzling phenomenon.

The third term, *anarchic*, intends to signal that the antithetical agency in which the being of the devil is and is exhausted has no independent "positive" aim or end or accountable purpose; that aimless dynamic is exhausted in its opposition to and contradiction of

18 Karl Barth, *Table Talk*, recorded and ed. John D. Godsey, *Scottish Journal of Theology Occasional Papers* 10 (Oliver and Boyd, 1963), 72. Cf. *Church Dogmatics* III/3 where Barth develops his account of *das Nichtige* as an ontologically "third" thing, not a creation of God's "yes" but an "effect" of God's implicit "no," the specification of what God "rejects."

19 Pseudo-Dionysius, *The Divine Names* 4.19, in *The Complete Works of Pseudo-Dionysius*, trans. Colm Luibheid (Paulist, 1987), 85.

God and God's good purposes and acts.[20] Polish philosopher Leszek Kolakowski expresses this insight forcefully when he writes:

> Satan himself only appears where destruction has no purpose, where cruelty and humiliation are perpetrated for their own sake, death for the sake of death, where suffering is without an end or where the end is only a mask worn to rationalize the hunger for destruction. Only there, however small be the setback to being, does the icy power reveal itself, a power which cannot be reduced to anything, explained by anything, justified in any way.[21]

We might also wish to take the meaning of *an*-archic in the other direction to suggest that the devil also has no proper origin, no positive originating principle. It is of nothing.

In sum, what I want to suggest is that something like the privative account of evil might be repurposed within the more dramatic and dynamic context of the second article of the creed. When translated here, however, this "privation" takes on a more concrete form as the specific negation and opposition to the saving work of God in Christ, naming the virulent and vicious enemy of the redemptive work of grace. It is from this working that we infer these claims about the nature of its being and action, claims we might digest into a single claim: namely, that the devil has a merely *an-ontological* or *antagontological* existence. That is an inelegant neologism if ever there were one. But perhaps we need an ugly and difficult term, a term seemingly itself at war with natural language, if we are aptly to designate the devil's absurd and contrary reality.

One specific question we might yet entertain is this: Is the devil a "person"? Ought we to speak of "personal evil" in speaking about the devil and all his works? In one sense I would have no objection to such talk. When we say the devil is a person, this is no less a metaphor—an improper but useful predication that helps us express something of the reality in question—than when we say the devil

20 Torrance, *Christian Doctrine of God*, 227: "Evil is essentially anarchic. It is an utterly irrational factor that has inexplicably entered into the created order. Whatever else evil is[,] it involves the introduction of a radical discontinuity into the world that affects the relation of [hu]mankind to God and humans with one another."

21 Leszek Kolakowski, "Shorthand Transcript of a Metaphysical Press Conference, Given by the Demon in Warsaw, on 20 December 1963," in *The Devil and Scripture*, trans. Celina Wieniewska (Oxford University Press, 1973), 130 (124–37).

is a "serpent" or a "dragon" or a "prince" or a "liar." In the case of "person," *qua* metaphor the term might draw attention to the *agential* character of evil, or pick out something about the *seemingly* intentional quality of diabolical resistance to God's ways and works, or gesture toward whatever kind of "stability" or discernible "pattern" might be glimpsed in its outworking, or point to a kind of identity worked out, as it were, in these antagonistic works. The "person" of the devil in this sense would gesture at the congealed yet viciously mobile contours of the void of evil. So far, so fine.

But pushed further, we might rightly balk at extending "personhood" to the devil if we mean it in any of the more careful or technical ways the term is deployed as a term of art in contemporary theology (proper) and/or theological anthropology. In chapter 5 I cited David Ford's judgment that in the Fourth Gospel the devil never properly becomes a full character in the story. The question we are asking just now presses into the reasons that might be so. Ironically, the devil is at his most "personal" when he is "least himself," i.e., as he becomes paradoxically identical with the figures of Peter and Judas in their intimate betrayals, as and when he is in closest proximity to the true person of Christ. Here he seems to win personal form only occasionally and parasitically. The matter is also made more complex when we recall how the designations "Satan" and "Devil" also work to pick out something horribly *legion*, "a colossal coalition" of antipathy and opposition to the movements of grace in the world.[22]

Further reflection on this issue could develop in various ways. We might, for example, pursue the idea that—with apologies to Melanchthon—"To know the devil is to know his deficits," meaning thereby that there is nothing substantive behind the operations of the devil, that his reality *just is* his *malificium*, i.e., that devilish being is fully identified with and exhausted in malevolent doing. Maybe like the figure in the line drawing by Rembrandt used on the cover of this book, the devil is an entirely transient reality, just briefly person-like, sketchily emerging only for a moment, only when "in act," i.e., only in active enmity with Christ's person and works. Such an account

[22] The phrase "colossal coalition" comes from J. J. van Oosterzee, *Christian Dogmatics*, vol. 2, trans. John Watson and Maurice J. Evans (Scribner, Armstrong & Co., 1874), 421.

would comport with claims I made a moment ago about the *an-ontological* quality of diabolical existence.

Yet another idea to pursue might be to construe the devil as a uniquely *anti-personal* reality, as does Robert Jenson, for example. Jenson suggests the devil is "a sort of negative, mirror-image person. He is a parasite-person . . . personal only in the passion of his refusal to be a person."[23] Joseph Ratzinger advances a similar line of argument when he asserts that the devil "is the Un-person, the disintegration and collapse of personhood."[24] The sense and summative force of such claims is clear enough in relation to the exposition I have advanced in these pages.

But perhaps an even looser account might in fact prove to be most apt. We might, for example, find something in the suggestion of the novelist David Adams Richards that Satan is a powerful "*condition* we come against," at once "nebulous," "profound" and frightening and ever "resolved to destroy faith."[25] Such a view would depersonalize the matter most fully. In such talk of the devil as an amorphous condition we might also hear an echo of the old idea of human bondage to sin as a condition, a comprehensive *vitium*, i.e., a powerful corruption "baked in" our circumstances which *vitiates* our capacity for faith and obedience, for love and honesty.[26] The idea of devil as an aggressively vitiating condition inimical to God and God's creatures is, to my mind, quite compelling, not least because it emphasizes well the sheer *antipathy in act* that marks the devil in our account. In any

[23] Robert Jenson, "Evil in Person," in *Theology as Revisionary Metaphysics: Essays on God and Creation*, ed. Stephen John Wright (Wipf and Stock, 2014), 140.

[24] Ratzinger, "Farewell to the Devil?" 204. Paul Tillich suggested that "personality is the most prominent object of demonic destruction." Paul Tillich, *The Interpretation of History* (Charles Scribner's Sons, 1936), 86.

[25] David Adams Richards, *God Is: My Search for Faith in a Secular World* (Anchor Canada, 2009), 106. The considerable power of this "condition" upon basic human trust and honesty—including honesty with ourselves—corrodes our most basic relations, undoing human community and fueling violence with hatred and fear. Richards's difficult fiction is devoted to narrating just this dissolution together with resistance to it, at once pedestrian and miraculous.

[26] Oliver Quick, *The Gospel of the New World* (Nisbet & Co., 1944), 47–48, reminds us that "the *vitium* of sin is the evil influence of past sins which renders the individual here and now unable to choose and do right. . . . The apocalyptists who followed the prophets were much more alive to the *vitium*." So too, perhaps, those students of the apocalyptists whose witness fills the New Testament.

case, all of these lines of thinking would rightly make refusing the devil proper personhood—whether as more than personal, or less than personal, or anti-personal, or impersonal—part of what is required by the faithful disbelief of Christians here.

§4 Discipleship before the enemy of Jesus Christ *par excellence*

Throughout this investigation I have been interested in gesturing toward ways in which fresh reflection upon the devil of the sort ventured here might bear upon our conception of the Christian life. Does the devil have a place in our doctrine of the Christian life, we might ask? There is much that could be said. For concision, I restrict myself to two indicative themes only: first, the notion of "living under providence," and second, the theme of resistance.

When dogmatic interest falls heavily upon the providential superintendence of devil as a matter of securing concerns in the first article—as is the case as we have seen in the traditional "majority report"—it funds strategies of Christian living that are resilient and supremely stoical in the face of evil, taking the "long view" as it were, invested in the power of the benevolence of God finally to put even the most devilish "permitted" evil to good ends.[27] However, prioritizing salvation over providence as a referential framework for the devil, as we have attempted to do here, allows the "logic" of the former (salvation) to control and administer the "logic" of the latter (providence). In this explicitly soteriological framing the devil is, as we have shown, primarily the adversary of God's saving purposes and the object of divine repudiation, denial, and defeat in the work of salvation itself. If we draw some of the concepts of providence forward into this framework, their meaning and significance are, I think, changed in important ways. When the logic of providence is ordered *under* the logic of salvation, then divine "permission" of evil comes to look less like a cool intellectual strategy for ensuring God is not the author of evil and instead invites being understood as purposeful divine patience in attack, something tactical, an enigmatic gambit in the divine campaign of saving grace. Similarly, the providential superintendence of devilish evil by God might then not be something affirmed coolly and propositionally in the "third person" but rather something sought in prayer and asserted in witness, something that takes concrete shape in the active resistance

[27] The Joseph story is paradigmatic here. Gen 50:20: "Even though you intended to do harm to me, God intended it for good . . ."

and repudiation of evil in and by the saving work of Christ and the ongoing witness of the Spirit *for us*.

Such shifts construe *our place* in the confrontation of God and evil differently and so orient us toward it differently. Providence—the arc of history that bends (even evil) toward justice—is long, eschatologically so; only in the eschaton will the providential governance of evil be fully and explicitly identical with the triumph of the saving lordship of Christ. In the meantime, shall we live in the face of evil primarily with patience in inscrutable providence, or shall we join ourselves with the salutary impatience of God displayed with evil in the saving work of the Redeemer? I imagine that the latter is enjoined upon the Christian life as a matter of faith in the gospel in a way that the former is not. In the time before providence and salvation manifestly align—in the time of what Paul Ricoeur styled the "broken dialectic" of Christian faith and life[28]—there is only the way of concrete discernment and struggle informed by the gospel and its entailments. What we are given and know is faith's own creaturely *agon* against the enmity of the devil and all his works, not as their ultimate solution—for that, as we have seen, is and could only be God's own business—but in a service and witness which arises in free and grateful response to Christ's invitation to become co-belligerents with him.

And so, briefly to resistance. Rowan Williams once remarked that "To some extent, the preaching of Jesus as Lord is a kind of parabolic drama: this is what happened, and you must discover where you stand."[29] An account of the saving lordship of Jesus in which the devil is firmly ingredient is a rehearsal of the drama of the gospel, a dogmatic retelling of "what happened." Heard as such, it can decisively inform our discerning just "where we stand" and so also who we are and what we might do. In the world remade around the person and work of Christ Jesus *agonistes*, the Christian life is lived out between "the fell incensed points / Of mighty opposites."[30]

[28] Paul Ricoeur, *Evil: A Challenge to Philosophy and Theology*, trans. John Bowden (Continuum, 2007), 59. Walter Sparn suggests that in the "interval between the 'already' and the 'not yet' the devil has a similar hermeneutical structure to the theological concept of tragedy." Sparn, "Über den Teufel," s.v.

[29] Rowan Williams, *On Christian Theology* (Blackwell, 2000), 97.

[30] *Hamlet*, Act V, scene 2, lines 61–62. C. S. Lewis alluded to this when he wrote on our theme: "There was never any question of tracing *all* evil to man; in fact, the New Testament has a good deal more to say about dark superhuman powers than

We have set out a series of brief remarks about the Christian life in the preceding chapters all under the overarching rubric and imperative: "Resist the devil, and he will flee from you" (Jas 4:7). I have suggested that the substance of the Lord's Prayer as well as our practices of baptism, the Lord's supper, Scripture reading, and proclamation, take on new concrete significance within the agonistic account of salvation our thinking about the devil has brought to light. This is premised on the idea that God does not contend with evil without affording beloved creatures and covenant partners "a share in the contention" as "co-belligerents."[31] Or in the words of one of the Christian poets of the last century, Jack Clemo, "To submit to God we must resist the devil. To obey the laws of heaven we must transgress the laws of hell. To be governed by divine predestination we must reject our natural fate as sinners."[32] Resistance is thus analytic in faithfulness, in discipleship; it is the concrete form vital faithfulness will take in the "still yet unredeemed world."[33] More specifically still, as I have suggested throughout, different aspects of the Christian life can be coordinated with specific modes of Christ's own saving confrontation with diabolical temptation, his overthrow of demonic possession, and his outbidding of devilish lies and betrayal. This concrete connection is what recommends the concept of "resistance" as a name for the essential dynamism of the life of faith.

If we think of the Christian life as a "parabolic life"—i.e., a life whose willing and doing can and should provide so many everyday parables of the eschatological gospel of our redemption—then we might imagine Christian activity in all its forms as ever so many and varied concrete "parables of resistance" to the devil and all his works.[34]

---

about the fall of Adam. As far as the world is concerned, a Christian can share more of the Zoroastrian outlook; we all live between the 'fell incensed points' of Michael and Satan." C. S. Lewis, "Evil and God," in *Undeceptions: Essays on Theology and Ethics*, ed. Walter Hooper (Geoffrey Blew, 1971), 3 (1–4).

31 Barth, *Church Dogmatics* III/3, 355; cf. p. 359: The human creature is "no mere spectator in this contest."

32 Clemo, *Invading Gospel*, 91.

33 The phrase is drawn from Article II of *The Theological Declaration of Barmen* (1934); see Douglas S. Bax, "The Barmen Theological Declaration: A New Translation," *Journal for Theology in Southern Africa* 47 (1984): 78–81.

34 See Philip G. Ziegler, "Parabolic Life: Toward an Ethics of God's Apocalypse," *Studies in Christian Ethics* 34, no. 4 (2021): 426–38.

We could then go on to ask about the emergent shape of human life caught up in Christ's saving confrontation and *agon* against the deathly enmity of evil. We can ask about and seek to discern ways of being in the world that will testify to Jesus's fidelity to his messianic vocation in the face of temptation. We can ask about and seek to discern ways of being in the world that will testify to his powerful repossession of depleted lives from death's occupation. And we can ask about and seek to discern ways of being in the world that will testify to his vindication of divine truth amidst betrayal and dissimulation. We can consider and advocate for the kinds of human actions and passions that will concretely resist the devil by resolutely refusing to disavow God's path of self-humbling for us as "The Way," by joyfully celebrating the dispossession of false and inhuman lordships by "The Life," and by honestly confessing both faith and sin in holding true and keeping faith with "The Truth."

Resisting despair in the face of evil, Christian discipleship means praying for, relying upon, hoping for, and trusting in that deliverance from the devil which only God can work—that "great exorcism" of the gospel of redemption—but to which we can in our all-too-human way correspond with our own active witness and service, even now. Christian ethics is then the disciplined task of reflectively discerning where, how, and when *this* battle is best joined by those who have received—and in faith now venture—their vocation as co-belligerents in the world and walk together in the train of the Crucified One. Moral theology thus becomes the science of militant faith, of impatient hope, and of faithful resistance. Of course, we cannot overdetermine these matters within our dogmatics in advance. For they belong most properly to the living endeavor of faith and life, of preaching and teaching, of discipleship and service in the ever-changing circumstances of individual lives and the lives of our communities. They are the stuff of discernment and adventure and so of risk and repentance. But our Christian doctrine can and should predispose and orient us in this discernment and adventure in ways that do better, rather than worse, justice to the gift and claim of the gospel of the Redeemer.

SOME FINAL QUESTIONS ARISING

At the outset of this short study I called to mind the program of Michael Welker's "new biblical theology" and its ambition to resharpen fundamental theological concepts long "dulled by multiple accommodations to prevailing habits of thought."[35] Perhaps this brief theology of the devil has, in its way, done something to resharpen the concept of the devil just a little and so to afford us a newly honed tool in the theological tool kit with which we work out our salvation in fear and trembling.

Being alert to the many ways such a tool might be used *and misused*, we must be on guard here against unwelcome affordances, e.g., irresponsible demonizing rhetoric by which political controversy and social disagreement can quickly be polarized and political opponents and social groups dehumanized—even and especially in times such as these.[36] Of course, to the extent that talk of the devil in Christian faith and life proves to be but the working out of our *ressentiment*, the projection of our wish fulfillment, or a means for mystifying the inhuman machinations of social, economic, or political power, then Christian theology can and should have none of it. If Elaine Pagels's ideological "social history" of the devil or Daniel Defoe's "political history" of the devil should turn out to be the only true and effective history of the figure there is—i.e., should our talk of the devil simply prove to be a rather overwrought way of saying "boo" to things that displease us greatly—then Christian theology can and should have none of it.[37]

But part of the wager of this book has been that the discipline of taking explicit responsibility for the devil in Christian theology affords us the best possibility of resisting the weaponization of the figure of the devil in the service of other ends, be they pernicious, irresponsible, or simply unthinking. Pursuit of a properly evangelical doctrine of the devil affords Christian theology invaluable critical and *self-critical* purchase upon the misuses and abuses of the discourse about the devil, including our own. Even so, as we have noted, in the end all our moral and dogmatic principles will not, as such, carry us victorious in *this* struggle. We should expect to find ourselves disoriented in the fog of this war, outflanked, and overrun and obliged time

35 Michael Welker, *Creation and Reality* (Fortress, 1999), 4.

36 On "affordances" see Ted Smith, *The End of Theological Education* (Eerdmans, 2023) and Hanna Reichel, *After Method: Queer Grace, Conceptual Design, and the Possibility of Theology* (Westminster John Knox, 2023).

37 Elaine Pagels, *The Origin of Satan* (Random House, 1995); Daniel Defoe, *The Political History of the Devil* (1726) (Nonsuch, 2007).

and again to acknowledge the immensity, virulence, and obscurity of evil and to be forced to confess our entanglement and complicity with it. Such discernment and confession require that the Christian struggle with the devil—both intellectual and practical, dogmatic and ethical—begin and end in humility, and repentance, and prayer. This posture of repentance and confession is the beginning and abiding essence of any truly holy resistance.

I hope this concise exploration of the figure of the devil as a renewed topic in Reformed theology and doctrine demonstrates the value of "tarrying with *this* negative" a little longer than one usually does, and of reframing Christian faith and life as something worked out amidst the redemptive *agon* of Christ against the adversary. Perhaps it affords us a way of hearing the martial idiom of the New Testament witness as good and important news, i.e., as a meaningful redescription of our world that provides some necessary purchase upon it we otherwise would not have. As one eminent Scottish divine reminds us: "In a day when spirit forces of passionate evil have been unleashed upon the earth and when fierce emotions are tearing the world apart, it is no use having a milk-and-water passionless theology. The thrust of the demonic has to be met with the fire of the divine. As indeed it can: since Christ has overcome the world."[38] Perhaps by attempting to think again in this refocused way about the inimical power Calvin called "God's adversary and ours," this brief dogmatic essay and experiment in diabology will help Christian faith and life and theology to see our bedeviled world illumined and transformed in the counterinsurgent light of that very divine fire.

[38] James Stewart, "On a Neglected Emphasis in New Testament Theology," *Scottish Journal of Theology* 4 (1951): 301.

BIBLIOGRAPHY

Acolatse, Esther E. *Powers, Principalities and the Spirit: Biblical Realism in Africa and the West*. Eerdmans, 2018.

Adler, Manfried, Corrado Balducci, and Hans Bender, et al. *Tod und Teufel in Klingenberg: Eine Dokumentation*. Paul Pattloch Verlag, 1977.

Albright, W. F. *From the Stone Age to Christianity*. 2nd ed. Doubleday/Anchor, 1957.

Allison, Dale C., Jr. "The Historians' Jesus and the Church." In *Seeking the Identity of Jesus: A Pilgrimage*, edited by Beverly Roberts Gaventa and Richard B. Hays, 79–95. Eerdmans, 2008.

Allison, Dale C., Jr. *The Jesus Tradition in Q*. Trinity Press International, 1997.

Anselm. *The Complete Treatises*. Edited and translated by Thomas Williams. Hackett, 2022.

Aquinas, Thomas. *On Evil*. Translated by Richard Regan. Edited by Brian Davies. Oxford University Press, 2003.

Aquinas, Thomas. *Summa Theologica*. Translated by Fathers of the English Dominican Province. Burns, Oates and Washbourne, 1927.

Augustine. *The City of God Against the Pagans*. Edited and translated by R. W. Dyson. Cambridge University Press, 1998.

Augustine. *The Enchiridion on Faith, Hope and Charity*. Translated by Boniface Ramsey. New City, 1999.

Augustine. *On the Nature of the Good*. In *Augustine's Early Writings*, edited and translated by J. H. S. Burleigh, 324–48. SCM, 1953.

Augustine. *The Trinity*. Edited and translated by Edmund Hill, OP. New City, 1991.

Aulén, Gustaf. *Christus Victor: An Historical Study of the Three Main Types of the Idea of the Atonement*. Translated by A. G. Herbert. SPCK, 1931.

Backus, Irena. "Demons." In *The Oxford Guide to the Historical Reception of Augustine*, edited by Karla Pollmann and Willemien Otten, 867–70. Oxford University Press, 2013.

Barclay, John. *Pauline Churches and Diaspora Jews*. Mohr Siebeck, 2011.

Barth, Hans-Martin. *Der Teufel und Jesus Christus in der Theologie Martin Luthers*. Vandenhoeck & Ruprecht, 1967.

Barth, Hans-Martin. "Zur inneren Entwicklung von Luthers Teufelglauben." *Kerygma und Dogma* 13 (1967): 201–11.

Barth, Karl. *The Christian Life*. Cornerstones. T&T Clark, 2017.

Barth, Karl. *Church Dogmatics*. Vols. 2–4. Edited by T. F. Torrance and G. W. Bromiley. Translated by T. F. Torrance, G. W. Bromiley, et al. T&T Clark, 1936–77.

Barth, Karl. *Table Talk*. Recorded and edited by John D. Godsey. *Scottish Journal of Theology Occasional Papers* 10. Oliver and Boyd, 1963.

Barton, Stephen C. "Johannine Dualism and Contemporary Pluralism." In *The Gospel of John and Christian Theology*, edited by Richard Bauckham and Carl Mosser, 3–18. Eerdmans, 2008.

Bauman, Zygmunt, and Leonidas Donskis. *Liquid Evil*. Polity, 2016.

Bax, Douglas S. "The Barmen Theological Declaration: A New Translation." *Journal for Theology in Southern Africa* 47 (1984): 78–81.

Beardslee, John W., III, ed. *Reformed Dogmatics*. Baker Book House, 1977.

Bell, Richard H. *Deliver Us from Evil: Interpretating the Redemption from the Power of Satan in New Testament Theology*. WUNT 216. Mohr Siebeck, 2007.

Best, Ernest. *The Temptation and the Passion: The Markan Soteriology*. 2nd ed. Cambridge University Press, 1990.

Böcher, Otto. *Christus Exorcista: Dämonismus und Taufe im Neuen Testament*. Kohlhammer, 1972.

Bohak, Gideon. *Ancient Jewish Magic: A History*. Cambridge University Press, 2008.

Bohak, Gideon. "Conceptualizing Demons in Late Antique Judaism." In *Demons and Illness from Antiquity to the Early-Modern Period*, edited by Siam Bhayro and Catherine Rider, 111–33. Brill, 2017.

Bohak, Gideon. "Jewish Exorcism Before and After the Destruction of the Second Temple." In *Was 70 CE a Watershed in Jewish History? On Jews and Judaism Before and After the Destruction of the Second Temple*, edited by Daniel R. Schwartz and Zeev Weiss, 277–300. Brill, 2011.

Bonhoeffer, Dietrich. *Discipleship*. Vol. 4 of *Dietrich Bonhoeffer Works*. Edited by Geffrey B. Kelly and John D. Godsey. Translated by Barbara Green and Reinhard Krauss. Fortress, 2003.

Bonhoeffer, Dietrich. *Ethics*. Vol. 6 of *Dietrich Bonhoeffer Works*. Edited by Clifford Green. Translated by Richard Krauss et al. Fortress, 2005.

Bonhoeffer, Dietrich. *Theological Education Underground, 1937–1940*. Vol. 15 of *Dietrich Bonhoeffer Works*. Edited by Victoria J. Barnett. Translated by Victoria J. Barnett et al. Fortress, 2012.

Boring, M. Eugene. *Mark: A Commentary*. New Testament Library. Westminster John Knox, 2006.

Bovon, Francois. *Luke 1: A Commentary on the Gospel of Luke 1:1–9:50*. Edited by H. Koester. Translated by Christine M. Thomas. Hermeneia. Fortress, 2002.

Bowens, Lisa M. *An Apostle in Battle: Paul and Spiritual Warfare in 2 Corinthians 12:1–10*. Mohr Siebeck, 2017.

Bradnick, David L. *Evil, Spirits, and Possession: An Emergentist Theology of the Demonic*. Global Pentecostal and Charismatic Studies 25. Brill, 2017.

Brown, Derek R. "The Devil in the Details: A Survey of Research on Satan on Biblical Studies." *Currents in Biblical Research* 9, no. 2 (2011): 200–27.

Brown, Raymond E. *The Community of the Beloved Disciple*. Paulist, 1979.

Brown, Raymond E. *The Gospel According to John (I–XII)*. Anchor Bible. Doubleday, 1966.

Brunner, Emil. *The Christian Doctrine of Creation and Redemption*. Translated by Olive Wyon. Lutterworth, 1952.

Buber, Martin. *The Eclipse of God: Studies in the Relation of Religion and Philosophy*. Harper & Row, 1952.

Bultmann, Rudolf. *The Gospel of John: A Commentary*. Translated by G. R. Beasley-Murray et al. Westminster John Knox, 1971.

Bultmann, Rudolf. *Theology of the New Testament*. Vol. 2. Translated by K. Grobel. Charles Scribner's Sons, 1955.

Cacciari, Massimo. *The Withholding Power: An Essay on Political Theology*. Translated by Edi Pucci. Bloomsbury, 2018.

Calvin, John. *Institutes of the Christian Religion* (1559). Translated by Ford Lewis Battles. Westminster, 1960.

Calvin, John. *Matthew, Mark and Luke: The Harmony of the Gospels*. Vol. 1. Edited by T. F. Torrance and D. W. Torrance. Translated by A. W. Morrison. Calvin's New Testament Commentaries. Eerdmans, 1994.

Carroll, John T. *Luke: A Commentary*. New Testament Library. Westminster John Knox, 2012.

Catechism of the Catholic Church. 2nd ed. United States Council of Catholic Bishops, 2019.

Chalamet, Christophe. "'Je suis le chemin, la vérité et la vie' (Jn 14,6)." *Revue d'Histoire et de Philosophie Religieuses* 99, no. 1 (2019): 99–111.

Cioran, Emil M. *The Trouble with Being Born*. Translated by Richard Howard. Arcade, 1976.

Clark, Stuart. *Thinking with Demons: The Idea of Witchcraft in Early Modern Europe*. Oxford University Press, 1999.

Clemo, Jack. *The Invading Gospel: A Return to Faith*. Marshall Pickering, 1986.

Conzelmann, Hans. *The Theology of St. Luke*. SCM, 1982.

Coyle, J. Kevin. *Manichaeism and Its Legacy*. Brill, 2009.

Culpepper, R. Alan. *The Gospel and Letters of John*. Abingdon, 1998.

daCosta, Jacqueline. "Evil in the Twenty-First Century." *Feminist Theology* 30, no. 2 (2022): 167–78.

Dahill, Lisa E. *Reading from the Underside of Selfhood: Bonhoeffer and Spiritual Formation*. Wipf and Stock, 2009.

Davies, Jamie. *The Apocalyptic Paul: Retrospect and Prospect*. Wipf and Stock, 2022.

Davies, Margaret. *Rhetoric and Reference in the Fourth Gospel*. A&C Black, 1992.

Davies, W. D., and Dale C. Allison. *Matthew 1–7*. T&T Clark, 1988.

Davies, W. D., and Dale C. Allison. *Matthew 8–18*. T&T Clark, 1991.

de Boer, Martinus C. "The Johannine Community Under Attack in Recent Scholarship." In *The Ways That Often Parted: Essays in Honor of Joel Marcus*, edited by Lori Baron, Jill Hicks-Keeton, and Matthew Thiessen, 211–41. SBL, 2018.

de Bruin, Tom. "In Defence of New Testament Satanologies: A Response to Farrar and Williams." *Journal for the Study of the New Testament* 44, no. 3 (2022): 435–51.

de Jonge, Henk J. "'The Jews' in the Gospel of John." In *Anti-Judaism and the Fourth Gospel*, edited by R. Bieringer, D. Pollefeyt, and F. Vandecasteele-Vanneuville, 121–40. Westminster John Knox, 2001.

De La Torre, Miguel A., and Albert Hernández. *The Quest for the Historical Satan*. Fortress, 2011.

Defoe, Daniel. *The Political History of the Devil* (1726). Nonsuch, 2007.

Dennison, James T., ed. *Reformed Confessions of the 16th and 17th Centuries in English Translation*. 4 vols. Reformation Heritage Books, 2008–14.

Denzinger, Heinrich. *Enchiridion Symbolorum: Compendium of Creeds, Definitions, and Declarations on Matters of Faith and Morals*. 43rd ed. Edited by Peter Hunermann. Ignatius, 2012.

Dorner, Isaak A. *A System of Christian Doctrine*. Vol. 3. Translated by Alfred Cave and J. S. Banks. T&T Clark, 1885.

Dow, Graham. *Explaining Deliverance*. Sovereign World, 2003.

Dow, Graham. *Those Tiresome Intruders: Sharing Experience in the Ministry of Deliverance*. Grove, 1991.

Eastman, Susan. *Oneself in Another: Participation and Personhood in Pauline Theology*. Wipf and Stock, 2023.

Eastman, Susan. *Paul and the Person: Reframing Paul's Anthropology*. Eerdmans, 2017.

Edwards, Ruth B. *Discovering John: Content, Interpretation, Reception*. 2nd ed. Eerdmans, 2014.

Farrar, Thomas J. "The Intimate and Ultimate Adversary: Satanology in Early Second-Century Christian Literature." *Journal for Early Christian Studies* 26, no. 4 (2018): 517–46.

Farrar, Thomas J. "New Testament Satanology and Leading Superhuman Opponents in Second Temple Jewish Literature: A Religio-Historical Analysis." *Journal of Theological Studies* NS 70, no. 1 (2019): 21–68.

Farrar, Thomas J., and Guy J. Williams. "Diabolical Data: A Critical Inventory of New Testament Satanology." *Journal for the Study of the New Testament* 39, no. 1 (2016): 40–71.

Farrar, Thomas J., and Guy J. Williams, "Talk of the Devil: Unpacking the Language of New Testament Satanology." *Journal for the Study of the New Testament* 39, no. 1 (2016): 72–96.

Ford, David. *The Gospel of John: A Theological Commentary*. Baker Academic, 2022.

Forsyth, Neil. *The Old Enemy: Satan & the Combat Myth*. Princeton University Press, 1987.

Frey, Jörg. "Dualism and the World in the Gospel and Letters of John." In *The Oxford Handbook of Johannine Studies*, edited by Judith M. Lieu and Martinus C. de Boer, 274–91. Oxford University Press.

Frey, Jörg. "Recent Perspectives on Johannine Dualism and Its Background." In *Text, Thought, and Practice in Qumran and Early Christianity*, edited by R. Clements and D. R. Schwartz, 127–57. Brill, 2023.

Fridrichsen, Anton. *Exegetical Writings: A Selection*. Edited and translated by Chrys C. Caragounis and Tord Fornberg. Mohr Siebeck, 1994.

Fröhlich, Ida. "Demons and Illness in Second Temple Judaism: Theory and Practice." In *Demons and Illness from Antiquity to the Early-Modern Period*, edited by Siam Bhayro and Catherine Rider, 81–96. Brill, 2017.

Fröhlich, Ida, and Erkki Koskenniemi, eds. *Evil and the Devil*. T&T Clark, 2013.

Fröhlich, Karlfried. *Gottesreich Welt und Kirche bei Calvin: Ein Beitrag zur Frage nach dem Reichgottesglauben Calvins*. Verlag Ernst Reinhardt, 1930.

Frye, Northrop. *The Great Code: The Bible and Literature*. Academic Press Canada, 1981.

Garrett, Susan R. *The Demise of the Devil: Magic and the Demonic in Luke's Writing*. Fortress, 1989.

Garrett, Susan R. *The Temptations of Jesus in Mark's Gospel*. Eerdmans, 1998.

Gaventa, Beverly Roberts. "Learning and Unlearning the Identity of Jesus from Luke-Acts." In *Seeking the Identity of Jesus: A Pilgrimage*, edited by Beverly Roberts Gaventa and Richard B. Hays, 148–65. Eerdmans, 2008.

Gaventa, Beverly Roberts. "The Rhetoric of Violence and the God of Peace in Paul's Letter to the Romans." In *Paul, John and Apocalyptic Eschatology*, edited by Jan Krans, Bert Jan Lietaert Peerbolte, Peter-Ben Smit, and Arie Zwiep, 61–75. Brill, 2013.

Gerrish, Brian. *The Christian Faith: Dogmatics in Outline*. Westminster John Knox, 2015.

Green, Kenneth Hart. *The Philosophy of Emil Fackenheim: From Revelation to the Holocaust*. Cambridge University Press, 2020.

Griffiths, Paul J. *Israel: A Christian Grammar*. Fortress, 2023.

Haenchen, Ernest. *John 2: A Commentary on the Gospel of John, Chapters 7–21*. Translated by Robert Funk. Hermeneia. Fortress, 1984.

Haering, Theodore. *The Christian Faith: A System of Dogmatics*. Vol. 1. Translated by John Dickie and George Ferries. Hodder & Stoughton, 1915.

Hauw, Andreas. *The Function of Exorcism Stories in Mark's Gospel*. Wipf and Stock, 2019.

Havel, Václav. *Living in Truth*. Edited by Jan Vladislav. Faber & Faber, 1986.

Havel, Václav. *Open Letters: Selected Writings, 1965–1990*. Edited by Paul Wilson. Knopf, 1991.

The Heidelberg Catechism in German, Latin, and English. Charles Scribner, 1863.

Heppe, Heinrich. *Reformed Dogmatics: Set Out and Illustrated from the Sources*. Translated by G. T. Thompson. Allen & Unwin, 1950.

Hodge, Charles. *Systematic Theology*. 3 vols. 1872–73. Repr., Eerdmans, 1981.

Jeffrey, David Lyle. *Luke*. Brazos Theological Commentary on the Bible. Brazos, 2012.

Jenson, Robert. "Evil in Person." In *Theology as Revisionary Metaphysics: Essays on God and Creation*, edited by Stephen John Wright. 136–45. Wipf and Stock, 2014.

Jervis, Ann. *Paul and Time*. Baker Academic, 2023.

John of Damascus. *On the Orthodox Faith*. Vol. 3 of *The Fount of Knowledge*. Translated by Norman Russell. St. Vladimir's Seminary Press, 2022.

Jones, Paul Dafydd. "Karl Barth on Gethsemane." *International Journal of Systematic Theology* 9, no. 2 (2007): 148–71.

Jüngel, Eberhard. *God as the Mystery of the World*. Translated by D. Guder. T&T Clark, 1983.

Kaftan, Julius Wilhelm. *Dogmatik*. 7th and 8th expanded ed. Mohr, 1920.

Kallas, James. *The Significance of the Synoptic Miracles*. SPCK, 1961.

Käsemann, Ernst. *On Being a Disciple of the Crucified Nazarene*. Translated by Roy Harrisville. Eerdmans, 2010.

Kazantzakis, Nikos. *The Last Temptation of Christ*. Translated by P. A. Bien. Faber and Faber, 1979.

Kelly, Declan. *The Defeat of Satan: Karl Barth's Three-Agent Account of Salvation*. T&T Clark, 2022.

Kelly, Henry Ansgar. *The Devil, Demonology, and Witchcraft: The Development of Christian Beliefs in Evil Spirits*. Rev. ed. Doubleday, 1974.

Kelly, Henry Ansgar. *Satan: A Biography*. Cambridge University Press, 2006.

Kelly, Henry Ansgar. *Satan in the Bible: God's Minister of Justice*. Wipf and Stock, 2017.

Kerr, Hugh T. *The First Systematic Theologian: Origen of Alexandria*. Princeton Theological Seminary, 1958.

Kierkegaard, Søren. *The Concept of Anxiety*. Edited and translated by Reidar Thomte. Princeton University Press, 1980.

Kim, Hyun Joo. *Bearing Sin as Church Community: Bonhoeffer's Hamartiology*. T&T Clark, 2022.

Kloppenborg Verbin, John. *Excavating Q: The History and Setting of the Sayings Gospel*. T&T Clark, 2000.

Koester, Craig R. "Jesus as the Way to the Father in Johannine Theology (John 14:6)." In *Theology and Christology in the Fourth Gospel*, edited by G. van Belle, J. G. van der Watt, and P. Maritz, 117–33. Peeters, 2005.

Kolakowski, Leszek. *The Devil and Scripture*. Translated by Celina Wieniewska. Oxford University Press, 1973.

Kotsko, Adam. *The Prince of this World*. Stanford University Press, 2017.

Kovacs, Judith L. "'Now Shall the Ruler of This World Be Driven Out': Jesus' Death as Cosmic Battle in John 12:2–36." *Journal of Biblical Literature* 114, no. 2 (1995): 227–47.

Krötke, Wolf. *Sin and Nothingness in the Theology of Karl Barth*. Edited and translated by Philip G. Ziegler and Christina-Maria Bammel. Studies in Reformed Theology and History NS 10. Princeton Theological Seminary, 2005.

Leonhardt-Balzer, Jutta. "The Ruler of the World, Antichrists and Pseudo-Prophets: Johannine Variations on an Apocalyptic Motif." In *John's Gospel and Intimations of Apocalyptic*, edited by Catrin H. Williams and Christopher Rowland, 180–99. T&T Clark, 2013.

Levinas, Emmanuel. *Of God Who Comes to Mind*. Translated by Bettina Bergo. Stanford University Press, 1998.

Lewis, C. S. "Evil and God." In *Undeceptions: Essays on Theology and Ethics*, edited by Walter Hooper, 1–4. Geoffrey Blew, 1971.

Lincoln, Andrew T. *Truth on Trial: The Lawsuit Motif in the Fourth Gospel*. Hendrickson, 2000.

Ling, Trevor. *The Significance of Satan: New Testament Demonology and Its Contemporary Relevance*. SPCK, 1961.

Löfstedt, Torsten. *The Devil, Demons, Judas, and "The Jews": Opponents of Christ in the Gospels*. Wipf and Stock, 2021.

Loftin, Matt. "Political Demons." *Christian Century* 142, no. 2 (2025).

Lombard, Peter. *Sentences*. Book 2, *On Creation*. Translated by Giulio Silano. PIMS, 2008.

Luther, Martin. *The Career of the Reformer IV*. Vol. 34 of *Luther's Works*. Edited and translated by Lewis W. Spitz. Muhlenberg Press, 1960.

Luz, Ulrich. *Matthew 1–7: A Commentary*. Translated by Wilhelm C. Linss. T&T Clark, 1990.

Luz, Ulrich. *Matthew 8–20: A Commentary*. Translated by James E. Crouch. Hermeneia. Fortress, 2001.

Lyons, Fintan, OSB. *The Persistence of Evil: A Cultural, Literary and Theological Analysis*. T&T Clark, 2023.

MacKinnon, Donald M. "Atonement and Tragedy." In *Borderlands of Theology and Other Essays*, edited by George W. Roberts and Donovan E. Smucker, 52–58. Lutterworth, 1968.

MacKinnon, Donald M. "Prayer, Worship, and Life." In *Philosophy and the Burden of Theological Honesty: A Donald MacKinnon Reader*, edited by John C. McDowell, 55–66. T&T Clark/Continuum, 2011.

Manson, T. W. "Principalities and Powers: The Spiritual Background of the Work of Jesus in the Synoptic Gospels." *SNTS Bulletin* 3 (1952): 7–16.

Marcus, Joel. *Mark 1–8*. Anchor Bible. Doubleday/Yale University Press, 2000.

Marcus, Joel. *Mark 8–16*. Anchor Bible. Yale University Press, 2009.

Mariani, Antonio Francesco. *The Life of St. Ignatius Loyola, Founder of the Jesuits*. 2 vols. Thomas Richardson and Son, 1849.

Marion, Jean-Luc. *Prolegomena to Charity*. Translated by Stephen E. Lewis. Fordham University Press, 2002.

Martyn, J. Louis. "The Apocalyptic Gospel in Galatians." *Interpretation* 54, no. 3 (2000): 246–66.

Martyn, J. Louis. "Epilogue: An Essay in Pauline Meta-ethics." In *Divine and Human Agency in Paul and His Cultural Environment*, edited by J. Barclay and S. Gathercole. T&T Clark, 2008.

Martyn, J. Louis. *Galatians*. Anchor Bible. Doubleday 1997.

Martyn, J. Louis. "The Gospel Invades Philosophy." In *Paul, Philosophy and the Theopolitical Vision: Critical Engagements with Agamben, Badiou, Zizek and Others*, edited by D. Harink, 13–36. Wipf and Stock, 2010.

Martyn, J. Louis. *History and Theology in the Fourth Gospel*. 3rd ed. Westminster John Knox, 2003.

Martyn, J. Louis. "World Without End or Twice-Invaded World?" In *Shaking Heaven and Earth: Essays in Honor of Walter Brueggemann and Charles B. Cousar*, edited by Christine Roy Yoder et al., 117–32. Westminster John Knox, 2005.

Mauser, Ulrich W. *Christ in the Wilderness: The Wilderness Theme in the Second Gospel and Its Basis in the Biblical Tradition*. SCM, 1963.

McGill, Alan. "A Truth Best Told Through Fiction: On Developing the Catholic Presentation of the Doctrine of Satan as a Mythic Probe into the Possible." PhD diss., University of Birmingham, 2015.

McRobert, Laurie. "Emil L. Fackenheim and Radical Evil: Transcendent, Unsurpassable, Absolute." *Journal of the American Academy of Religion* 58, no. 2 (1989): 325–40.

Methodius. *The Symposium*. Translated by Herbert Musurillo. Longman, Green and Co., 1958.

Miller, Samantha L. *Chrysostom's Devil: Demons, The Will, and Virtue in Patristic Soteriology*. IVP Academic, 2020.

Moltmann, Jürgen. "Zwölf Bemerkungen zur Symbolik des Bösen." *Evangelische Theologie* 52, no. 1 (1992): 1–6.

Morse, Christopher. *The Difference Heaven Makes: Rehearing the Gospel as News*. T&T Clark, 2010.

Mottu, Henry. "Bonhoeffer and Our Theological Existence Today." In *A Bonhoeffer Legacy*, edited by A. J. Klassen, 204–12. Eerdmans, 1981.

Mühlethaler, Daniel. *Der Teufel wider den trinitarischen Gott in der Theologie Martin Luthers*. Evangelische Verlangsanstalt, 2024.

Myers, Ched. *Binding the Strong Man: A Political Reading of Mark's Story of Jesus*. 20th anniversary ed. Orbis, 2008.

Neiman, Susan. *Evil in Modern Thought*. Princeton University Press, 2002.

Nemo, Philippe. *Job and the Excess of Evil*. Duquesne University Press, 1998.

O'Connor, Flannery. *Mystery and Manners: Occasional Prose*. Farrar, Straus & Giroux, 1969.

O'Day, Gail R. "Miracle Discourse and the Gospel of John." In *Miracle Discourse in the New Testament*, edited by Duane F. Watson. 175–88. SBL, 2012.

O'Gara, Margaret. *The Ecumenical Gift Exchange*. Liturgical, 1998.

Obendiek, Harmannus. *Der Teufel bei Martin Luther*. Furche Verlag, 1931.

Oberman, Heiko. *Luther: Man Between God and the Devil*. Translated by Eileen Walliser-Schwarzbart. Yale University Press, 1989.

Onyinah, Opoku. "Spiritual Warfare: The Cosmic Conflict Between Good and Evil." In *The Routledge Handbook of Pentecostal Theology*, edited by Wolfgang Vondley, 321–31. Routledge, 2020.

Origen, *Against Celsus*. Translated by Henry Chadwick. Cambridge University Press, 1965.

Osborne, B. A. E. "Peter: Stumbling-Block and Satan." *Novum Testamentum* 15, no. 3 (1973): 187–90.

Otto, Rudolph. *The Kingdom of God and the Son of Man: A Study in the History of Religion*. Translated by F. V. Wilson and B. L. Woolf. Lutterworth, 1938.

Pagels, Elaine. *The Origin of Satan*. Random House, 1995.

Pagels, Elaine. "The Social History of Satan, Part II: Satan in the New Testament Gospels." *Journal of the American Academy of Religion* 62, no. 1 (1991): 17–58.

Pagels, Elaine. "The Social History of Satan, the 'Intimate Enemy': A Preliminary Sketch." *Harvard Theological Review* 84 (1991): 105–28.

Painter, John. "Monotheism and Dualism: John and Qumran." In *Theology and Christology in the Fourth Gospel*, edited by G. van Belle, J. G. van der Watt, and P. Maritz, 225–43. Peeters, 2005.

Pascal, Blaise. *Pensées*. Edited by Léon Brunschvicg. Gallimard, 1897.

Patočka, Jan. *The Selected Writings of Jan Patočka: Care for the Soul*. Edited by Ivan Chvatník and Erin Plunkett. Translated by Alex Zucker. Bloomsbury, 2022.

Pedersen, Daniel J. *Schleiermacher's Theology of Sin and Nature: Agency, Value, and Modern Theology*. Routledge, 2020.

Piper, Ronald A. "Satan, Demons and the Absence of Exorcisms in the Fourth Gospel." In *Christology, Controversy and Community: New Testament Essays in Honour of David R. Catchpole*, edited by David G. Horrell and Christopher M. Tuckett, 253–78. Brill, 2000.

Pope Francis. *Gaudete et Exsultate* (March 19, 2018). https://www.vatican.va/content/francesco/en/apost_exhortations/documents/

papa-francesco_esortazione-ap_20180319_gaudete-et-exsultate.html.

Pseudo-Dionysius. *The Complete Works of Pseudo-Dionysius*. Translated by Colm Luibheid. Paulist, 1987.

Quick, Oliver. *The Gospel of the New World*. Nisbet & Co., 1944.

Ratzinger, Joseph. "Farewell to the Devil?" In *Dogma and Preaching*, edited by Michael J. Miller, translated by Michael J. Miller and Matthew J. O'Connell, 197–205. Ignatius, 2011.

Reichel, Hanna. *After Method: Queer Grace, Conceptual Design, and the Possibility of Theology*. Westminster John Knox, 2023.

Reynolds, Bennie H., III. "Demonology and Eschatology in the Oppositional Language of the Johannine Epistles and Jewish Apocalyptic Texts." In *The Jewish Apocalyptic Tradition and the Shaping of New Testament Thought*, edited by Benjamin E. Reynolds and Loren T. Stuckenbruck, 327–45. Fortress, 2017.

Richards, David Adams. *God Is: My Search for Faith in a Secular World*. Anchor Canada, 2009.

Richards, David Adams. "I Will Show You Fear in a Handful of Dust." *Vision: A Journal for Church and Theology* 20, no. 1 (2019): 29–34.

Ricoeur, Paul. *Evil: A Challenge to Philosophy and Theology*. Translated by John Bowden. Continuum, 2007.

Ridderbos, Herman N. *The Gospel According to John: A Theological Commentary*. Translated by John Vriend. Eerdmans, 1997.

Rigby, Cynthia L. "Evil and the Principalities: Disarming the Demonic." In *Life amid the Principalities: Identifying, Understanding, and Engaging Created, Fallen, and Disarmed Powers Today*, edited by Michael Root and James J. Buckley, Pro Ecclesia 6, 327–45. Wipf and Stock, 2016.

Rohls, Jan. *Reformed Confessions: Theology from Zurich to Barmen*. Translated by John Hoffmeyer. Westminster John Knox, 1998.

Runciman, Steven. *The Medieval Manichee: A Study of the Christian Dualist Heresy*. Cambridge University Press, 1947.

Russell, Jeffrey Burton. *The Devil: Perceptions of Evil from Antiquity to Primitive Christianity*. Cornell University Press, 1977.

Russell, Jeffrey Burton. *A History of Heaven: The Singing Silence*. Princeton University Press, 1997.

Russell, Jeffrey Burton. *Mephistopheles: The Devil in the Modern World*. Cornell University Press, 1986.

Russell, Jeffrey Burton. *Satan: The Early Christian Tradition*. Cornell University Press, 1987.

Schaff, Philip. *The Harmony of the Reformed Confessions, as Related to the Present State of Evangelical Theology*. Dodd, Mead & Co, 1877.

Schleiermacher, F. D. E. *The Christian Faith*. Translated by H. R. Mackintosh. T&T Clark, 1928.

Schleiermacher, F. D. E. *The Life of Jesus*. Edited by Jack C. Verheyden. Translated by S. Maclean Gilmour. Fortress, 1975.

Scott-Macnab, David. "Augustine's Trope of the Crucifixion as a Trap for the Devil and Its Survival in the English Middle Ages." *Viator* 46, no. 3 (2015): 1–20.

Shakespeare, William. *Hamlet: Revised Edition*. The Arden Shakespeare. Bloomsbury, 2016.

Shakespeare, William. *The Merchant of Venice*. The Arden Shakespeare. Bloomsbury, 2011.

Shively, Elizabeth. *Apocalyptic Imagination in the Gospel of Mark: The Literary and Theological Role of Mark 3:22–30*. De Gruyter, 2012.

Simon, Edward. *Pandemonium: A Visual History of the Devil*. Abrams/Cernunnos, 2022.

Smith, D. Moody. *The Theology of the Gospel of John*. Cambridge University Press, 1995.

Smith, Ted. *The End of Theological Education*. Eerdmans, 2023.

Sonderegger, Katherine. *Systematic Theology I: The Doctrine of God*. Fortress, 2015.

Sparn, Walter. "Über den Teufel." In *Religion in Geschichte und Gegenwart*, 4th ed., edited by Hans Dieter Betz, Don S. Browning, Bernd Janowski, and Eberhard Jüngel. Mohr Siebeck, 2007.

Stewart, James. "On a Neglected Emphasis in New Testament Theology." *Scottish Journal of Theology* 4 (1951): 292–301.

Stoyanov, Yuri. *The Other God: Dualist Religions from Antiquity to the Cathar Heresy*. Yale University Press, 2000.

Stuckenbruck, Loren T. "Evil in Johannine and Apocalyptic Perspective: Petition for Protection in John 17." In *John's Gospel and Intimations of Apocalyptic*, edited by Catrin H. Williams and Christopher Rowland, 200–232. T&T Clark, 2013.

Stuckenbruck, Loren T. "Satan and Demons." In *Jesus Among Friends and Enemies: A Historical and Literary Introduction to Jesus in the Gospels*, edited by Chris Keith and Larry W. Hurtado, 173–97. Baker Academic, 2011.

Taubes, Jacob. *Occidental Eschatology*. Translated by David Ratmoko. Stanford University Press, 2009.

Taylor, Charles. *A Secular Age*. Harvard University Press, 2007.

Tertullian. *Apology*. Translated by T. Herbert Bindley. Parker and Co, 1890.

Thavis, John. *The Vatican Prophecies: Investigating Supernatural Signs, Apparitions, and Miracles in the Modern Age*. Viking, 2015.

Thielicke, Helmut. *Fragen des Christentums an die Moderne Welt*. Mohr, 1947.

Thielicke, Helmut. *Man in God's World: The Faith and Courage to Live—or Die*. Translated by J. W. Doberstein. James Clarke, 1967.

Thigpen, Paul. *Saints Who Battled Satan*. TAN, 2015.

Thomas, Gabrielle. "Basil of Caesarea and Gregory of Nazianzus on the Role of the Devil in Problems of Evil and Suffering." *International Journal of Systematic Theology* 26, no. 4 (2024): 351–66.

Thomas, Gabrielle. *The Image of God in the Theology of Gregory of Nazianzus*. Cambridge University Press, 2019.

Thomas, Günter. "Sin and Evil." In *The Oxford Handbook of Karl Barth*, edited by Paul Dafydd Jones and Paul T. Nimmo, 354–72. Oxford University Press, 2019.

Thompson, Marianne Meye. *The God of the Gospel of John*. Eerdmans, 2001.

Thompson, Marianne Meye. *John: A Commentary*. New Testament Library. Westminster John Knox, 2015.

Tillich, Paul. *The Interpretation of History*. Charles Scribner's Sons, 1936.

Tonstad, Sigve K. "'The Father of Lies,' 'The Mother of Lies,' and the Death of Jesus (John 12:30–33)." In *The Gospel of John and Christian Theology*, edited by Richard Bauckham and Carl Mosser, 193–208. Eerdmans, 2008.

Torrance, Thomas F. *The Christian Doctrine of God: One Being Three Persons*. T&T Clark, 2016.

Turretin, Francis. *Institutes of Elenctic Theology*. Vol. 1. Edited by J. T. Dennison Jr. Translated by George Musgrave Giger. P&R, 1992.

Twelftree, Graham H. *Jesus the Exorcist: A Contribution to the Study of the Historical Jesus*. Mohr Siebeck, 1993.

van der Watt, Jan G. "Salvation in the Gospel According to John." In *Salvation in the New Testament: Perspectives on Soteriology*, edited by H. J. Bernard Combrink and Jan G. van der Watt, 101–31. Brill, 2005.

van Oosterzee, J. J. *Christian Dogmatics*. Vol. 2. Translated by John Watson and Maurice J. Evans. Scribner, Armstrong & Co., 1874.

van Oudtshoorn, André. "Where Have All the Demons Gone? The Role and Place of the Devil in the Gospel of John." *Neotestamentica* 51, no. 1 (2017): 65–82.

Vatican. "Christian Faith and Demonology." *L'Osservatore Romano*, English ed., July 10, 1975, 6–10.

Vogel, Heinrich. *Gott in Christo: Ein Erkenntnisgang durch die Grundprobleme der Dogmatik*. Teil 2, *Heinrich Vogel Gesammelte Werke*. Band 2. Radius Verlag, 1982.

Volf, Miroslav. "Johannine Dualism and Contemporary Pluralism." In *The Gospel of John and Christian Theology*, edited by Richard Bauckham and Carl Mosser, 19–50. Eerdmans, 2008.

Warfield, Benjamin Breckinridge. "The New Testament Terminology of 'Redemption.'" In *Biblical Doctrines*, vol. 2 of *The Works of Benjamin B. Warfield*, 327–74. Repr., Baker Book House, 1981.

Wassén, Cecilia, and Tobias Hägerland. *Jesus the Apocalyptic Prophet*. T&T Clark, 2021.

"Weapons of the Devil: Hibakusha's Call for a World Without Nuclear Weapons." *American Friends Service Committee*, August 5, 2015. https://afsc.org/news/weapons-devil-hibakushas-call-world-without-nuclear-weapons.

Webster, John. *Holy Scripture: A Dogmatic Sketch*. Cambridge University Press, 2003.

Weil, Simone. *First and Last Notebooks*. Translated by Richard Reese. Oxford University Press, 1970.

Welker, Michael. *Creation and Reality*. Fortress, 1999.

Wiebe, Gregory D. *Fallen Angels in the Theology of St. Augustine*. Oxford University Press, 2021.

Wilder, Amos. *Jesus' Parables and the War of Myths*. Fortress, 1982.

Williams, Rowan. *On Christian Theology*. Blackwell, 2000.

Wingren, Gustav. *Theology in Conflict: Nygren, Barth, Bultmann*. Translated by E. H. Wahlstrom. Muhlenberg Press, 1958.

Wolter, Michael. *Das Lukasevangelium*. Mohr Siebeck, 2008.

Wüthrich, Matthias D. "An Entirely Different Theodicy: Karl Barth's Interpretation of Human Suffering in the Context of his Doctrine of *das Nichtige*." *International Journal of Systematic Theology* 23, no. 4 (2021): 593–616.

Wüthrich, Matthias D. *Gott und das Nichtige: Zur Rede vom Nichtigen ausgehend von Karl Barths KD §50*. Theologischer Verlag, 2006.

Yarbro Collins, Adela. *Mark: A Commentary*. Edited by Harold Attridge. Hermeneia. Fortress, 2007.

Yates, Roy. "Jesus and the Demonic in the Synoptic Gospels." *Irish Theological Quarterly* 44, no. 1 (1977): 39–57.

Ziegler, Philip G. "The First and Final 'No': The Finality of the Gospel and the Old Enemy." In *The Finality of the Gospel: Karl Barth and the Tasks of Eschatology*, edited by Kaitlyn Dugan and Philip G. Ziegler, 193–213. Brill, 2022.

Ziegler, Philip G. *Militant Grace: The Apocalyptic Turn and the Future of Christian Theology*. Baker Academic, 2018.

Ziegler, Philip G. "Parabolic Life: Toward an Ethics of God's Apocalypse." *Studies in Christian Ethics* 34, no. 4 (2021): 426–38.

INDEX OF SUBJECTS

INDEX OF NAMES

INDEX OF BIBLICAL AND ANCIENT SOURCES